A PLEA
FOR THE ABOLITION OF TESTS
IN THE UNIVERSITY
OF OXFORD

This is a volume in the Arno Press collection

THE ACADEMIC PROFESSION

Advisory Editor
Walter P. Metzger

Editorial Board
Dietrich Goldschmidt
A. H. Halsey
Martin Trow

See last pages of this volume
for a complete list of titles.

A PLEA

FOR

THE ABOLITION OF TESTS

IN THE

UNIVERSITY OF OXFORD

GOLDWIN SMITH

ARNO PRESS

A New York Times Company

New York / 1977

Editorial Supervision: **MARIE STARECK**

———◆———

Reprint Edition 1977 by Arno Press Inc.

Reprinted from a copy in
  The University of Michigan Library

THE ACADEMIC PROFESSION
ISBN for complete set: 0-405-10000-0
See last pages of this volume for titles.

Manufactured in the United States of America

———◆———

Library of Congress Cataloging in Publication Data

Smith, Goldwin, 1823-1910.
    A plea for the abolition of tests in the University of
Oxford.

    (The Academic profession)
    Reprint of the 1864 ed. published by Wheeler & Day,
Oxford.
    1. Oxford. University—Examinations. I. Title.
II. Series.
LF504.S5 1977   378.16'6'0942574   76-55201
ISBN 0-405-10026-4   *77- 9253*

A PLEA

FOR

THE ABOLITION OF TESTS.

A PLEA

FOR

THE ABOLITION OF TESTS

IN THE

UNIVERSITY OF OXFORD,

BY

GOLDWIN SMITH.

SECOND EDITION,

OXFORD:

WHEELER AND DAY.

LONDON: HAMILTON AND CO,

1864.

OXFORD:

T. COMBE, M.A., E. PICKARD HALL, AND H. LATHAM, M.A.

PRINTERS TO THE UNIVERSITY.

PREFACE.

As the writer was one of those who signed the Petition presented to Parliament last Session for the Abolition of Tests, he feels it due to the rest of those who signed, to say that the following pages express his own views and sentiments alone. He has not written in concert with, or with the knowledge of, any other person.

It may be as well here to state briefly the existing Law.

The Act 17 and 18 Vict. c. 81, abolished all Oaths and Declarations at Matriculation and on taking the degree of Bachelor in Arts, Law, or Medicine. But by the Statutes of the University no person can take the degree of Master or Doctor, or become a member of Convocation, the governing body of the University*, without subscribing the Thirty-nine Articles, and, in addition, the three Articles of the 36th Canon, the same which are subscribed by the Clergy at their Ordination, and the second of which, pledging the person subscribing " to use the forms prescribed in the Book of Common Prayer and Administration of the Sacraments, and none other," is properly applicable to Clergymen alone.

Degrees in Theology are confined by the Statutes of the University to persons in Priests' Orders.

By the Act of Uniformity all Heads and Fellows of Colleges, among other persons, are required, at their admission, to make a declaration of Conformity to the Liturgy of the Church of England.

In most of the Colleges the Fellows are obliged, either by the College Statutes or by the Ordinances of the late Commission, to take the

---

* The Cambridge Act enables persons to take the Master's degree without the Tests, but not to become members of the governing body.

degree of M. A. or one of the Superior degrees, for which, as before stated, subscription to the Thirty-nine Articles and the three Articles of the 36th Canon is required. In other Colleges, the Fellowships are expressly confined either by their own Statutes, or by the Ordinances of the Commission, to Members of the Church of England. In some cases both provisions occur. In one case only, it is believed, the limitation of the Fellowships to Members of the Church of England rests on the Act of Uniformity alone.

The Act 17 and 18 Vict. authorises persons to open Private Halls for the reception of Students, with a license from the Vice-Chancellor. But the Master of a Private Hall must be a Member of Convocation, and must therefore have taken the Tests.

OXFORD, January 21, 1864.

A PLEA

FOR

THE ABOLITION OF TESTS.

A PETITION from members of the University of Oxford for the abolition of tests of religious opinion on admission to academical degrees was presented to both Houses of Parliament last Session. It was signed by 106 persons, two of whom were Heads of Colleges, while the rest were or had been connected, as Professors, Tutors, or Fellows, with University or College government and education. The petition was presented in the House of Lords by Earl Russell, in the House of Commons by Mr. Dodson. Its prayer was supported in the Upper House by Earl Granville and the Bishop of London, and in the Lower House by Mr. Buxton, Mr. Grant Duff, and Mr. Göschen. Mr. Gladstone, without actually supporting the prayer of the petition, commended the question, as one requiring attention, to the consideration of the University, and went so far as to intimate his own opinion that the stringency of the present tests was in the case of laymen, at least, open to reasonable objection.

The opponents of the petition directed their arguments more against the manner in which it had been got up, than against its actual prayer, or the reasons by which its prayer was supported. It will scarcely be thought presumptuous to claim for the persons whose names were appended to it credit for not having intentionally done anything insidious or unfair towards their opponents *. Those of them especially who are clergymen, and who know well what obloquy they incur in their own profession, and how their professional prospects may be affected, by a declaration in favour of liberty of conscience, have, in signing the petition, given a sufficient guarantee at least for their integrity and courage. The changes which the document underwent were not intended to mislead opponents, but were such as documents intended to be signed by a large number of persons, who, though agreed as to their main object, may differ in details, are very apt to undergo. An anxiety to make the petition as little open to misconstruction as possible, especially on religious grounds, will scarcely be imputed as a fault to the framers. And it was certainly not by any contrivance or in accordance with any wish of the petitioners that the presentation was postponed till very near the end of the Session of Parliament, when it was scarcely possible that a question of importance should be effec-

---

* I believe I am justified in stating that the Vice-Chancellor wrote to Lord Derby, assuring him that though the time when the petition was presented might be thought inconvenient to its opponents, no suspicion of any insidious intention on the part of the petitioners could be entertained. Mr. Henley's misstatements, couched in language indicative of their levity, may safely be allowed to find their own level.

tively discussed, and quite impossible that the discussion should result in legislation.

The number of those who signed the petition must be compared, as Mr. Gladstone justly remarked, not with that of Convocation at large, but with that of the much smaller body of men who hold or have held headships, professorships, fellowships, or tutorships, and have thus not merely possessed the academical franchise, but been really connected with the University. It must also be regarded, as Mr. Gladstone emphatically avowed, not merely as a stationary quantity, but as indicative of a growing feeling in the University; in which, twenty years ago, probably not a tenth of the number would have been found ready to sign such a petition. And further, the number of clerical signatures must be estimated as having been obtained in the face of a hostile feeling on the part of the clergy generally, falling little short of professional terrorism, which vents itself in the gravest imputations against teachers of Christianity convicted, by their own act, of believing that reason and conscience, when left unfettered by political tests, will bear free witness to Christian truth.

It has been said that the petitioners ought to have applied in the first instance to the University; and that they were guilty of a breach of academical loyalty in going at once to Parliament for relief. No one can feel more strongly than the writer of these pages, no one, when there was occasion, has asserted more earnestly the expediency of keeping the great places of national education independent of the political government of

the country and of the influences by which, especially
under the system of Party, that government is controlled. No one can be more sensible of the evils
which arose, both to the University and the nation,
when Oxford, the common heritage of Englishmen,
became, through unhappy accidents, the miserable tool
of the Jacobite faction; and which would again arise
if ever she should be made the tool of a similar faction
again. But as regards the present question, it is to
be observed, in the first place, that these tests were,
in fact, imposed from without by the arbitrary exercise
of a political power which was then vested in the Crown
and exerted through Chancellors nominated by the
Sovereign, but which has now passed into the hands
of the Legislature, and carried with it the responsibility
for the maintenance of the tests. In the second place,
it is to be observed that to the University, in the
proper sense of the term, it is idle to apply, since
she is not a free agent in the matter. The great
majority of Convocation consists of clergymen not
resident at Oxford, nor much touched by academical
needs or sympathies, who come on these occasions
to vote—and can be little blamed for voting—with
a single eye to the objects and interests, necessarily
and perhaps rightly paramount in their minds, of
the clerical profession. To ask such a Convocation to repeal religious tests would seem rather
like an act of ironical mockery, especially if the inevitable refusal were to be followed by an appeal to
Parliament, than like a tribute of allegiance and
respect.

What is it that actually takes place when these
questions are brought before us in Convocation? The
term before last, the Council proposed a petition
against Mr. Bouverie's bill for enabling colleges, if
they thought fit, to admit candidates to fellowships
without tests of religious opinion. When Convocation
assembled it was evident that the members really
engaged in the work of the University, to whom arguments founded on the claims of academical industry
and the expediency of extending the benefits of the
University, might have been addressed with some hope
of success, and with not a few of whom such arguments did in fact prevail, were swamped by clergymen having only clerical objects and interests, whom
such arguments would not only have failed to move,
but perhaps have hardened in their determination. It
was therefore of little consequence, that, by a strained
construction (as many thought) of the mediæval statute forbidding us to speak in English, we were denied liberty of debate, and compelled to agree not
only to the prayer of the petition, but to a whole
string of what appeared to opponents very questionable reasons, without discussion and in the lump.

Parliament has already taken the subject in hand.
It has interposed so far as to abolish the tests at
Matriculation, and on the Bachelor's degree, and thus
to save us for the future from the crime (for it de-
serves no milder name) of oppressing and corrupting,
for political purposes, the consciences of boys. But
this measure of relief, in favour of which not only a
regard for morality, but almost the voice of decency

and humanity might seem to plead, was opposed by the clerical party in the University, and by the allies of that party in the House of Commons. Much more would the same party oppose and defeat any further measure of emancipation, if it were brought forward within the University in the manner which our opponents prescribe.

We are not guilty then of any disrespect towards the University, or of any want of regard for her real independence, in making our appeal to statesmen for her emancipation from restrictions which we sincerely believe to be injurious to her utility and greatness as a national place of "religion, learning, and education."

The statesmen to whom the appeal will be made will not be those who are indifferent to the first of these three objects. On the contrary, some of the arguments to be tendered are such as no statesman could entirely appreciate who had not grasped the truth, which is as much one of political philosophy as of Revelation, that religion is the foundation of society. At the same time, to entertain any proposal of change a man must, no doubt, be so far a liberal as to be willing to submit all human institutions (from the number of which religious restrictions imposed by the Legislature, or by the Crown, will scarcely be excepted) to the test of reason and morality; and to believe it possible, at least, that the progress of society, continued through all the ages, may not have been arrested for ever at the exact point at which the present generation stands. And, in the same way, it is of course idle to plead for liberty of any kind to a

man who has made up his mind, on grounds supposed
to be above reason and conscience, that all desire of
liberty is rebellious wickedness, and that the preva-
lence of such a desire is a sign that the nations are
given over to the Spirit of Evil, and that the world
is drawing towards its end.

There are two questions at issue, in principle distinct
from each other, which it is necessary to a right
understanding of the subject, and the fairest course
towards our opponents, to discuss separately, though
they are intimately connected together, and may perhaps practically run into one. The first question relates to the maintenance of the existing tests. The
second question relates to the confinement of the
Universities, or at least of their higher honours,
franchises, and emoluments, to the members of the
Established Church. The system of exclusion might
be maintained in full force with less stringent tests
than the present, or indeed without any test at all.
England and Spain are now, it is believed, the only
countries in which the Universities are not free *. In
Spain, besides the general security given by the penal
suppression of all religions but that established by the
State, each candidate for admission is, or was till
lately, required to produce a certificate from a priest.
Such a certificate, if demanded of every candidate
for the higher degrees, or for a fellowship in the
University of Oxford, would fully serve the purpose
of exclusion: and it might be given by the priest

* The Universities are free in our Colonies. England alone is
thought unworthy of this measure of liberty.

without putting any actual test of doctrine, from his personal knowledge of the candidate's character as a faithful and obedient member of the Church.

In fact, proposals for relaxing the stringency of the tests have actually been made by some of those who think it necessary to maintain the system of exclusion. These persons perceive the immorality of the present system; and if their measures of concession do not obtain more support among their friends, it is mainly perhaps because their friends feel that tests of religious opinion have been generally condemned by the sense, conscience, and experience of mankind, and that though it may be possible, in a certain condition of political parties, to cling to those which remain, it would be impossible, if these were abandoned, to enact new tests in their place.

In truth, who can look the present system fairly in the face without seeing at once that it is immoral? A man presents himself to receive the final reward of his industry as a student, a reward in which the friends who have supported him at the University have an interest as well as himself, and the renunciation of which involves not merely the direct loss of the degree or fellowship *, but the fatal stamp of social nonconformity and of an eccentric mind. You contemplate the possibility of his being unwilling to subscribe to such a mass of doctrine as the Thirty-nine Articles, either from a doubt as to its being

---

* Subscription to the Thirty-nine Articles is not necessary for election to a fellowship : but it is necessary in most cases for holding one ; Fellows generally being required (as was stated in the Preface) to take the M.A. degree.

unmixed truth, or simply because he feels that it is his duty to God to keep his conscience free: otherwise there would be no need of tests at all. Yet you call upon him to subscribe as the condition of his receiving the reward. Do you not hereby wilfully and deliberately tempt him, by the bribe of worldly advantages, and the threat of worldly degradation, to lie to God and to his own soul? Such a system may serve the political interests of an Establishment, but is it possible that it can serve the spiritual interests of the Christian Church? Can it long stand before the awakened moral sense of mankind? If we were not made callous by official custom and party casuistry, should we fail to perceive that no imaginable sin against the God of Truth can be greater or more deadly than that of deliberately corrupting the spirit of truth in a young heart?

The Articles contain several hundred propositions of Theology. They bear upon them throughout the evident marks of the element of doubt and controversy out of which they arose*. They are in their nature an attempt to settle questions of opinion by an arbitrary exercise of political power: and those by whom the power was wielded were men, to say the least, actuated more by motives of state than by motives of

---

* It need hardly be said that the Sixth Article, which asserts that there *never was any doubt* in the Church as to the authority of any book of our Canon, is a most sinister monument of the controversial exigencies of the framers. The same thing may be said of the opening sentence of the Preface to the Ordination Service,—" It is evident unto all men diligently reading the Holy Scriptures and ancient authors, that from the Apostles' time there have been these orders of Ministers in Christ's Church ; Bishops, Priests, and Deacons." The word *diligently* seems to betray a consciousness of the character of the statement.

religion, and whose characters were such that it would
be not so much an absurdity as a blasphemy to suppose
that their spiritual perceptions could supersede the
voice of God in conscience as the criterion of religious
truth. The imposition of the Articles on Oxford is
historically connected with the name of the Earl of
Leicester, then our Chancellor, a villain assuredly,
and probably the murderer of his wife. Parliament
itself, which, so far as the laity were concerned,
was, and still is, the legal imponent, ratified these
formularies only after considerable discussion ; and even
then limited subscription to those Articles " which *only*
concern the confession of the true Christian faith and
the doctrine of the sacraments," a limitation which
was arbitrarily disregarded in practice by the bishops *.
Who can pretend to be assured that formularies so
framed, under such circumstances, and by such hands,
are absolute and final truth ? If we have no assurance
that they are absolute and final truth, how can it

* It was on this occasion that a remarkable conversation passed
between Mr. Wentworth, the most distinguished assertor of civil liberty
in the House of Commons, and Archbishop Parker. " I was," says
Wentworth, " among others the last Parliament sent for unto the
Archbishop of Canterbury, for the articles of religion that then passed
this house. He asked us ' why we did put out of the book the articles
for the homilies, consecration of bishops, and such like.' 'Surely, Sir,'
said I, 'because we were so occupied in other matters that we had no
time to examine them how they agreed with the word of God.' ' What,'
said he, ' surely you mistake the matter, you will refer yourselves
wholly to us therein ! ' ' No, by the faith I bear to God,' said I, ' we
will pass nothing before we understand what it is, for that were but to
make you popes : make you popes who list,' said I, ' for we will make
you none.' See Hallam, Const. Hist. chap. iv.

be just to impose them upon the consciences of men?
And what true policy can bid us outrage justice?

Is it to secure unanimity of opinion on religious
subjects in the Universities that the legislature imposes
these tests? If so, we have an argument against the
continuance of the system, the validity of which statesmen never fail to recognize. Decisive experience has
shown that the tests entirely fail to secure the object
for which they were instituted. There is not unanimity
but the greatest diversity of opinion, in the Universities: and this diversity extends, the advocates of the
present system themselves being witnesses, not merely
to secondary questions, but to the fundamental principles of faith *. The division is not kept secret, but
is displayed in fierce controversies and mutual persecutions. Nor is it only of to-day or yesterday. It
appeared with equal violence in the times when the
Arminians, headed by Laud, were contending with
the Puritans for the possession of Oxford. It has appeared alike at every period when intellect has been
active and conscience has been awake. It has slum-
bered only in seasons when intellectual torpor and
spiritual indifference prevailed in the University, in
the Church, and in the nation at large.

What new error or heresy is it feared that Oxford
will produce if conscience is unfettered? Is it feared
that she will produce Roman Catholics? Is it feared
that she will produce Free Thinkers? Do not the very
facts which are cited by the advocates of the tests to

---

* " We do not believe in the same God," says Dr. Pusey to Mr. Wilson,
who has, equally with himself, taken all these tests.

scare us from emancipation prove conclusively that
the evils which it is said would arise from freedom,
exist in their most dreaded form under the present
system? And is it not among the clergy, who are
doubly and trebly bound by tests, rather than among
the less fettered laity, that these evils arise?

Is it not wonderful that this should be the case.
By forcing a mass of questionable doctrine upon the
now awakened consciences of men at an early period
of life, you can hardly fail to produce in their minds
a premature uneasiness and restlessness on these subjects. By tyrannizing over conscience you can hardly
fail to arouse a rebellion against your tyranny which
will probably be carried by the sense of wrong far
beyond the bounds of rational resistance.

The test fails to promote, or rather tends to defeat,
the object with which it was instituted. It is felt as
a great grievance by a large number of persons. Can
there be a more complete case in the eye of a statesman for remedial legislation?

We shall be told, perhaps, by a certain school
among our opponents, that the Church guarantees to
us the truth of the Articles, and absolves conscience
from all need of inquiry, and from all risk of com-
mitting a sin by unhesitating acquiescence. We are
bound at least to ask, What Church? If the visible
Church, the patent fact is that even according to the
estimate of high Anglicans, who exclude Protestants
from the Church, and include only themselves, the
Roman Catholics, and the Greeks, an overwhelming
majority of the visible Church rejects the Thirty-nine

Articles, and pronounces that they are not only not pure truth, but fraught with deadly error. If the invisible Church, we are of course put to the inquiry, What the invisible Church is, and, further, how it came to be embodied in the Parliaments of Elizabeth and Charles II? If the national Church, we shall have to ask by what passage of Scripture, or by what principle of reason, authority is given to a mere political and geographical section of Christendom to bind and loose conscience by its decisions over a certain area, and to make that truth on one side of the Channel which, by an analogous authority, might be made falsehood on the other. The vision of Englishmen has been enlarged beyond the narrow island boundary by which it was confined in Tudor times; it takes in other Christian countries; and the claims of the Established Church of this island on our unquestioning allegiance are now judged, not by the tone of authority in which she prefers them, but by her position among the Churches of Christendom. Nor has history failed to do its part by uncrowning the despots of the past, and reducing to the stature of men, and men of very disputable character and wisdom, those half divine personages who could once impose themselves as the authorised exponents of divine truth on the reverence of a prostrate nation.

Parliament at all events has not regarded subscription to the Articles as a mere act of unreasoning submission to Church authority; for by a statute, of which the measure now sought would be merely an extension, it has done away with subscription at Matriculation and

on taking the Bachelor's degree. The ground on which
this measure of concession received the support of several
Conservatives was, that candidates for Matriculation or
for the Bachelor's degree were too young to have satis-
fied their minds by study and inquiry as to the truth
of the doctrines to which they were called upon to
subscribe. People cannot be too young, too ill informed,
too deficient in intellectual capacity or in the mature
sense of responsibility for an act of mere submission to
the authority of the Church. The argument used to
justify the abolition of subscription to the Articles in
this case applies equally to the cases of all persons
who, whether from their youth or from the nature
of their duties in life, have not had time or opportunity to master the enormous mass of controversial
divinity which the Articles comprehend. But the
acknowledgment of its validity by Parliament in any
case shows that in the contemplation of the Legislature, the real imponent of these tests, subscription is
not merely a blind act of submission, but an act of
reason and conscience, only to be justified, or required,
on reasonable and conscientious grounds.

The Articles themselves take the same view. They
refer to Scripture as the ultimate standard of religious
truth: and of course it must be, not the mere written
or printed characters of the Bible, but Scripture read
by the reasons and consciences of men. The singular
document prefixed to the Articles, called ' His Majesty's
Declaration,' will be found to look in the same direction. It sets forth indeed, in sufficiently strong terms,
the right and duty of kings, as national popes, to

order the consciences of their subjects and to keep
all men in the unity of the true (that is of the royal)
religion. But it appeals distinctly, though incidentally,
to a ground of acquiescence different from that of mere
filial submission to authority, whether it be the authority of the Church embodied in Convocation, of the
Church embodied in a Convocation of clerical digni-
taries, or of the Church embodied in Parliament.
" For the present, though some differences have been
ill raised, yet we take comfort in this, that all clergymen within our realm have always *most willingly*
subscribed to the Articles established ; which is an
argument to us, that they all *agree* in the true, usual,
literal meaning of the said Articles ; and that even in
those curious points, in which the present differences
lie, men of all sorts *take the Articles of the Church of
England to be for them ;* which is an argument again
that none of them intend any desertion of the Articles
established." This is not exactly an appeal to reason
or conscience : perhaps some might think it an appeal
to a motive of a very different kind. But it clearly
implies that assent to the Articles on a ground distinct from that of mere submission to authority is
a matter of satisfaction to the imponent.

It is well known that casuistical expedients of va-
rious kinds have been invented to make the Articles
easier of digestion to reluctant minds. The most
singular of them, perhaps, looking to experience, is
the attempt to construe these formularies as Articles
of Peace. No party in the Church has taken advantage of such loopholes for an uneasy conscience more

largely, or has stood more manifestly in need of them, than those who are now most resolute in forcing the Articles in the most stringent sense on the consciences of others. For all are aware that those who are the great enemies of free inquiry in general were not long since, and indeed may be said still to be, the great friends of that particular kind of free inquiry which, when logically and boldly conducted, leads ultimately, and has already in many cases led, to a rejection of the Anglican Church in favour of the Church of Rome. It was to coerce this party, by precluding the evasive constructions under which they eluded the law, that the authorities of the University proposed, some time since, to ascertain, by a rigid interpretation, the meaning of subscription : and the proposal was resisted by the party on the rather ominous ground, that the University might be itself mistaken in the interpretation which it proposed to affix. But if these expedients are tendered to us as palliatives of our case, or put forward as an answer to our complaints, we must be permitted to say that liberty of prevarication is to honest men no liberty at all, and that the recognition of such subterfuges, (if they are recognized,) only proves that immediate emancipation is demanded in the interest of every cause which has not bid farewell to ordinary morality. The same thing may be said of all exhortations to put yourself, by an effort of moral compliance, in the frame of mind in which the Articles will seem tolerably true. Such a process is simply an abandonment of truth ; and would lead a man to acquiesce, not only in the Thirtynine Articles, but in any kind of superstition.

The Petition before mentioned, points to the evil effect of the present system in producing a looseness of conscience and a habit of tampering with solemn obligations. Who can doubt that this is the case? And who can doubt that the sight of men subscribing to religious formularies under such circumstances, and with such suspicions attaching to their act, is much more calculated to spread infidelity, in the deepest and worst sense of the term, among those who witness it, than to confirm them in any kind of faith?

A petition was got up against Mr. Bouverie's Bill, and signed by upwards of a thousand Undergraduates, praying that no alteration might be made in the existing law. The advocates of the present system, both in Parliament and in the press, attached great importance to this document, as showing that a large number of those who had not yet taken the tests, looked forward to doing so, not only without any sense of hardship, but with entire satisfaction. Important the document unquestionably was. Judging from the regular course of study in this place, it may be very safely said, that of the undergraduates who signed the petition, the majority had not studied the formularies in question: some probably had not even read them through with attention, if they had read them through at all. Yet they were all ready to sign a petition praying that these formularies might continue to be imposed, not only on their own consciences, but on the reluctant consciences of others. Suppose this had taken place among the students of some dissenting University, or in any community reputed heterodox, should we not have been called upon to mark the effects of a bad system in begetting want of reverence for conscience, and levity in matters of religious truth* ?

A clerical member of the University suspected of heterodoxy may be called upon by the Vice-Chancellor to repeat his subscription to the Thirty-nine Articles† : and this instrument of moral torture has of late been brought into play. Nobody supposes that any object worthy the name of religious is gained by the proceeding. Nobody supposes that the suspected person is at all better affected to the doctrines of the Articles after repeating his subscription than he was before. Nobody feels that any further assurance of his orthodoxy has really been given to any human being. Persecution, and attempts to drive the supposed heretic from the University by insult and injustice, go on after the pretended act of satisfaction, just as they did before. One object only has been attained, the open degradation of an opponent. This interpretation, and this interpretation alone, is put upon the proceeding on all hands : and whether the feeling produced in the minds of the beholders be that of malignant exultation, or of generous disgust, the effect on the interests of religion is the same.

---

* For an account of this Petition and for the argument based on it, see the Bishop of Oxford's speech in the House of Lords, in the debate on the Petition for the Abolition of Tests, July 3, 1863.

† Whether it could be done in the case of a layman seems doubtful. The words of a penal statute would of course be construed strictly.

These tests are the vestiges, the last lingering vestiges, of an age of religious tyranny and oppression of
conscience—an age when the best of Christians and
of citizens, guilty of no offence but that of loving
the truth, and desiring to impart it to their brethren,
were treated as felons, harassed, fined, thrust into
noisome dungeons and kept there till they died, at
the instigation of ecclesiastics who dishonoured the
Christian name, and by the hands of politicians who
equally dishonoured it, and who in many cases had no
convictions whatever of their own—when the eucharist
itself, the bond of Christian love, was prostituted to
the purposes of political hatred with the appro-
bation of a so-called Christian clergy, though with a
profanity worse, because deeper in its nature, and
polluting holier things, than the impieties of the
ignorant heathen—when, in Scotland, many a peasant,
merely for worshipping God in the way he thought
the best, was shot down by a godless soldiery hounded
on by bishops styling themselves the successors of
the Apostles—when Ireland was oppressed by a penal
code which bribed the child to apostasy by enabling
him, as a reward, to strip his father of his property,
and not only of his inherited property, but of that
which he might himself acquire—when immorality and
infidelity went hand in hand with spiritual slavery,
and, while Baxter and Calamy lay in prison for their
convictions, obscene plays were being acted in the
harem of a Defender of the Faith, who lived a careless
infidel, mocking at morality and God, and who died a
craven infidel, calling in his panic for the viaticum of

c 2

superstition. Is not that age, with all that belonged
to it, numbered with the past? Are not its practices
disclaimed even by those who have not yet eradicated
its sentiments from their hearts? Have not all men
capable of profiting by any experience whatever, pro-
fited by the experience which, recorded in characters
more terrible than those of blood, tells us that conscience cannot be forced, that God will accept none
but a free allegiance, and that reason, and reason
alone, is our appointed instrument for bringing each
other to the truth? Can any one imagine that the
suppression of differences of opinion, which the great
powers of the earth, seated on its most ancient and
awful thrones, failed to effect with their united force,
will be effected by a party born but yesterday, and
still unsettled in its own opinions, with so miserable a
fragment of that force as an academical test? Why
should we, the great body of the English people,
who have no interests to serve but those of truth and
sincere religion, any longer oppress, vex, and harass
the consciences of each other? Why should we thus
aggravate the religious perplexities and distresses which
are gathering fast enough around us all? If it is for
a political object that we do this, how can true policy
be divorced from justice? If it is for a religious
object, how can religion consist with depravation of
conscience? If it is for the sake of the clergy, will
not a desire to see them really influential and truly
useful as spiritual guides lead us at once to take out
of their hands these instruments of self-degradation,
by the use of which they are alienating from them-

selves the moral sense as well as the intellects of men?

One remark more must be made before we leave this part of the subject. Political and academical tests, such as we seek to abolish, are totally different things from terms of spiritual communion or qualifications for spiritual office. This is the answer to those who are disposed to confront the advocates of political or academical emancipation with charges of laxity in doctrine or indifference to religious truth. It is not proposed to alter the Articles, or to relax in any way the canon of orthodox doctrine required by the Church, as a Church, either on the part of her communicants or on the part of her clergy. All that is proposed is to remove tests imposed by political power on candidates for literary and scientific degrees. It is the more necessary to insist on this, because the confusion of ideas against which the remark is intended to guard, seems to have found its way into the mind, or at least into the language, of a very eminent man. Mr. Gladstone is reported to have said in the debate on the Petition, that "he could not conceive how, with a system of religious truth purporting to be revealed and essentially definite, you could separate the propagation of tests from the principle and maintenance of that religion." "It seemed to him like dividing the bone from the flesh, so that vitality itself must escape in the severance." And he went on to argue that as the Apostles' Creed, which was a primitive document, was in the nature of a test, tests must have been sanctioned by the

usage of the Primitive Church. Whether dogmatism
and exclusiveness have their source in the writings of
the Apostles, or whether they are not traceable rather
to the Byzantine and Roman than to the Apostolic
mind, is a question which we need not here discuss.
Nor need we inquire whether there is anything on
the face of the Apostles' Creed to show that it was
intended to be used otherwise than as a summary of
faith.   If there were theological formularies equivalent
to the Thirty-nine Articles and the Athanasian Creed
in the days of the Apostles, it is certain that there
were no political tests.   Or rather there were political tests, which some of the Apostles and many of
their followers were put to death for refusing to
take.

   The spiritual strictness of a Church indeed is likely
to be rather in inverse than in direct proportion to
the stringency of its political tests, and to the degree
of support which it receives generally from political
power.   For such support is, and must be, pur-
chased by corresponding concessions to the powers of
the world : not only by making the Church à political
tool in their hands, but by allowing them to use it
as a cloak for their own moral and religious license
so long as they promote its apparent interests by
oppressing and persecuting its opponents.   It may
safely be said that no Christian Church, we might
almost say no heathen association which made any
pretension to a bond of religious union, has ever been
so loose with regard to spiritual requirements and terms
of communion as the Church of England was in the

reign of Charles II, when, supported by the full power
of a tyrannical government, she was allowed to mul-
tiply political tests in supreme scorn of conscience,
and held Nonconformist ministers imprisoned in every
gaol. To the period of intolerance and persecution
naturally succeeded a period of general scepticism.
During this period, was the eucharist, as a qualification for office, refused to scoffers at Christianity?
And can we imagine a more deplorable or a more
instructive union of political tyranny with spiritual
laxity, than the administration of the eucharist to an
unbeliever as a qualification for office would afford?
Bolingbroke, at once an infidel and a persecutor of
Nonconformists, was in fact the lay head of the Church
in his day, and might have communicated, if he
deigned to communicate, on any terms he pleased :
and generally speaking, any one who will look over
the history of the Established Church will see that
she has seldom been independent enough to ask what
were the religious convictions or what was the character
of her political chief. The same thing may be said,
with at least equal force, of the Churches established
by the State in Roman Catholic countries. The
Church of the Dragonades was the Church of Dubois ;
and it formed at once the terror of sincere Nonconformity and the decent veil of royal and aristocratic
lust. Men of the world, in fact, have found by
experience that a Church supported by political power,
and dependent on that support, is the best antidote
to the active influence of religion, which they choose
to regard as a dangerous and disturbing element in

society; and in paying their homage and lending their protection to a State religion, whether it be that of Jupiter or that of the Anglican Church, they are actuated partly by this view, and partly by the belief that the clergy are useful as a police. The kingdom of the Author of Christianity, after all, is not a kingdom of this world; nor can the kingdoms of this world be made those of the Author of Christianity by the process of political legislation, though they may, and, as we believe, will be in the end, by a process of religious conversion.

And so, on the other hand, it must not be supposed that those who most desire the removal of these tests, and of all interference of political power with conscience, seek to impugn, in any way, the spiritual integrity of the Anglican Church, or to force her to abandon anything which she holds to be an essential part of her proper duty as the guardian of religious truth. They may hope—some of them certainly do hope—that when, the hand of political power being withdrawn, the Churches of Christendom cease to be divided by political and social barriers from each other, and to be shut up each in the legal creeds and formularies imposed on it by the State, charity and the sense of a common life derived from the same sources and producing essentially the same fruits, will work their way through the hard integument of exclusive dogma in which each State Church is cased: and that a reconciliation, if not a reunion, of Christendom, will ultimately take place. But they expect this result from conscience, reason, and Christian sympathy, not from political compromise : and they are as far as possible from wishing to liberalize any Church by legislative action—above all by the action of a Parliament which has lost the last vestige of a title to legislate in matters of religion—or to force any Church to surrender for the convenience of secular interests any portion of what it deems the truth.

We now come to the distinct question as to the opening of the Universities to Dissenters. Dissenters or Nonconformists they shall be called here; to avoid multiplying issues. But if liberty of conscience be the principle of English society, the proper name of these communities is not Dissenters but Free Churches.

The relations between Church and State, and the rights as citizens of persons not belonging to the Anglican Church, are a subject on which it has become necessary that statesmen, if they would be worthy of the name, should at least have some definite principle distinctly before their minds. In the times of the Tudors, when the relations between Church and State were settled, and in the time of Charles II, when that settlement was restored, it was assumed that Church and State were one, and that conformity and citizenship were coextensive : nor did the aristocratic revolution which is associated with the name of William III. alter the principle, although it qualified the practical rigour of intolerance ; and although the State, led by political exigencies, to which its so-called religious principles invariably yield, accepted, at the union with Scotland, the absurd and fundamentally sceptical position of

establishing one religion on the North, and another
on the South of the Tweed. The Nonconformists were
persecuted under the Tudors and the Stuarts : under
William and his successors they were tolerated; and
the measure of toleration was enlarged as they grew
in numbers and in influence, and as, by the softening
influence of time on religious antipathies, and by the
gradual diffusion of free thought in Europe, their
enemies, the fanatical clergy, lost hold on the power of
the State. But under neither dynasty were they regarded as entitled to the rights of citizens, or as placed
in any other than a penal condition, the penalties of
which the State, out of mercy or policy, was pleased to
mitigate or suspend. At the same time it must be
remembered that no statesman of the Tudor age, or
even of that which succeeded the Tudors, looked upon
this state of things as perpetual, or supposed that a
large part of the nation would always remain politi-
cally and socially cut off, as Nonconformists, from the
rest, deprived wholly or in part of the privileges of
citizens, and therefore malcontent and disaffected.
These politicians were in fact misled, in a great measure, by their passionate desire to produce perfect
national unity, and their inability to understand that
perfect national unity might exist notwithstanding
diversities in religion. The complete identity of Church
and State, of churchman and citizen, which they regarded and propounded as the ideal polity, they also
fully expected to realise in fact. They more or less
definitely looked upon Nonconformity as a transient
malady, which would disappear in the end, provided

the rulers of the State persevered in the system of
encouraging the Established Church and discouraging
all others. Such was their expectation even with regard
to Ireland, where their theory and the ecclesiastical
law in which it was embodied were most signally and
most obstinately confronted by adverse facts. What
were their ideas as to the relations of the State Church
of England to the other Churches of Christendom;
whether they expected that the whole Christian world
would in the end be converted to the doctrines of the
Thirty-nine Articles, the last revision of the Prayer-
Book, and the Homilies, or whether they were content
that each Christian nation should continue to have
its own national religion, and consequently its own
national God, after the fashion of polytheistic antiquity,
it would probably be difficult to determine. They were
not men of high spiritual aspirations or of very ample
vision in the spiritual sphere : and their chief aim was
the complete subordination of the people to the purposes of the government, and the consolidation of a
great and compact power. When a philosophical mind
undertook to supply a religious basis to their political
theories, the result was such as the concluding books
of Hooker's Ecclesiastical Polity display.

It is now for statesmen to determine whether the
experience of three centuries is not conclusive as to
the vanity of these expectations : whether there remains
any ground whatever for hoping that Nonconformity
will cease, and that national unity will be brought
about by the adherence of all citizens to the Anglican
religion. In forming their opinion they will consider

not only the relative numbers of Churchmen and Nonconformists, Protestant or Catholic, at the present day,
but the relative increase of their numbers respectively
since the foundation of the Established Church. They
will balance not only the numbers or the numerical
increase, but the amount of religious energy displayed
by those who found and maintain free Churches by
their own efforts and at their own cost, notwithstanding
political penalties or disadvantages, compared with the
amount displayed by adherence to a Church endowed
and encouraged by the State. They will be careful,
especially with regard to the people of the rural districts, to distinguish between mere negative acquiescence, the result of ignorance or custom, and positive
conviction. They will also distinguish the results of
the social and educational efforts which the clergy
have made of late years, and in which they have been
supported by the wealth and influence of the Anglican
upper classes, from a renewed growth of Anglican doctrines in the minds of the people. They will examine
the internal condition of the Anglican Church itself,
and mark what is the degree of unity which it enjoys,
or is likely, to all appearances, to enjoy; and whether
its distinctive tenets really command the allegiance of
its most powerful and influential minds. Finally,
they will look abroad over Christendom, with the destinies of which it can scarcely be supposed that the
destinies of any Christian nation are wholly uncon-
nected, and see whether men are generally more inclined to make conscience bow before established
formularies, to sacrifice truth to political convenience,

or to reverence forms of religion imposed by the authority of kings. They will remember that in every nation of Europe where the powers of government were such as to lead rulers into arbitrary courses, the same attempt has been made to produce perfect unity in religion by the enforcement of conformity : and their own observation will tell them whether in every country of Europe the attempt has not decisively failed.

If they are brought to the conclusion that to produce national unity according to the Tudor plan, by forcing or inducing all the people to profess the State religion, has been proved to be hopeless, it only remains for them to seek the same end in another way, by recognising perfect liberty of conscience, by granting to all citizens the full privilege of citizenship, by finally renouncing on the part of the government pretensions which have led to nothing but disaster, and placing the State in what experience has shown to be its true position as the equal guardian of the secular rights and interests of all. If the old principle has failed, it ought, by all the rules of real statesmanship, to be frankly abandoned, and the new and sounder principle on which society is henceforth to stand ought to be cordially embraced. The advantages which practical wisdom, so called, sees in niggardly and extorted concession, are surely more than countervailed to the true statesman's eye by the bitterness of the strife, the long legacy of faction, the loss of the gratitude and harmony which attend a freely bestowed boon, the waste, in a barren and useless struggle, of power which might be expended in promoting the general good.

Toleration, which treated the Nonconformist half as a criminal, half as a citizen, was manifestly a transition state. The day of toleration is now past, the day of equality is come. Its coming will make us,—its approach has already begun to make us,—a more united, a more loyal, a more prosperous, and a more religious nation.

If the principle of religious equality is to be embraced, and all loyal citizens, whatever their religious creed, are to be accepted as in the full sense members of the nation, it would seem to follow as a matter of right and of course that they must all be admitted on equal terms to every national institution, and among others to the national Universities. You may try to temper the Nonconformist's exercise of his right, in the first instance at least, so as not to give an unnecessary shock to interests or sentiments which have grown up under the Tudor system. But you cannot deprive him of his right, without doing that which is the most unstatesmanlike of all things, an act of palpable injustice.

The only answer, apparently, that can be made to this claim of right is, that the Universities belong, not to the nation, but to the Anglican Church. And this, though it is not expressly stated, is constantly suggested or implied in the reasonings of the clerical party. It is plainly suggested in the Petition before mentioned as having been presented by the clerical party in the University against Mr. Bouverie's Bill.

Legally, the Universities are lay corporations. They are represented by Burgesses in the National Legislature. They are visited by the Crown in the Court of Queen's Bench. Their Chancellors may be and in modern times always have been laymen. Holy Orders are not required as a qualification for admission to their governing bodies or for any office in them, excepting those the holders of which must have taken Theological degrees.

The same is in truth the case in an historical point of view. No doubt the Universities in the middle ages had something of an ecclesiastical character. They were founded, or their foundation was confirmed, under Papal bulls, and the visitatorial power over them was the subject of contention between diocesans, metropolitans, and popes. In the proclamations of mediæval kings, regulating the relations between the students and the citizens of Oxford, the citizens as a body are sometimes called *Laici*, in contradistinction to the *Scholares*, who are assumed to be clerks. But all intellectual institutions in the middle ages were ecclesiastical. Society was in those times divided into the military class, the peasantry, the burghers, and the clergy : and the clergy comprehended not only those who were devoted to the cure of souls, but all who professed learning of any kind and wrought with the brain not with the hand, —the lawyer and the physician, the man of letters and the man of science, even the architect and the engineer. Wykeham the founder of New College was a bishop, and held a mass of clerical preferment: but he passed the early part of his life as an architect, and the latter part as a diplomatist and statesman. A clergyman in the modern sense of the term, as one devoted to pastoral duties or to theological study, he never was. And if we go deeper, and inquire to which of the two antagonistic elements of mediæval intellect the Universities belonged, to that which was sacerdotal and reactionary or to that which was scientific or progressive, we shall find the answer embodied in some of the most interesting facts of mediæval history. The Universities were the very centres of science and of progress : to the sacerdotal and reactionary party they were the objects of deserved suspicion. In them, during the thirteenth and fourteenth centuries, commenced the movement which issued at last in the great intellectual revolution of the sixteenth, called by the name, which, considering the variety of its effects, is inadequate, of the Protestant Reformation. To gain control over the seats of mental independence, the Dominicans and Franciscans threw themselves into the Universities in the thirteenth century, as the Jesuits threw themselves into the intellectual world in the sixteenth *. The most characteristic, as well as the most illustrious figures in the history of Oxford before the sixteenth century are Roger Bacon and Wycliffe : both of whom, under the strictly clerical dominion to which we have since become subject, have been regarded, we may say, with something of Dominican aversion †. The

* They fell themselves, in some cases, notably in the case of Roger Bacon, under the influence which it was their mission to combat.

† Bacon perhaps rather in the person of his more illustrious namesake than his own.

founder of our most ancient college, and the most
ancient of all colleges, Walter de Merton, was the
friend of Robert Grosteste, the liberal Bishop of
Lincoln, whose antagonism to the Roman and sacerdotal party gave rise to the statement, whether
literally true or not, that he died under excommu-
nication,—to Rome an ecclesiastical castaway, to English liberals a saint. And to the reforming party of the
reign of Henry III, to which both of these men belonged,
we owe not only the first loosening of the Roman
yoke, but, in no small degree, our Parliamentary institutions, the offspring of a spirit of political inquiry
which was fostered, together with the spirit of philosophic and scientific inquiry, in the Universities, and
found its expression in the Latin songs of the student
as well as in the deeds of De Montfort and his
companions in arms. Merton excluded monks from
his college : and the monks of those days were, in
point of reactionary spirit, the High Church clergy
of these. His Fellows were clerks, no doubt, but
seculars, not regulars : and the tendency of his regulations was to create a literary not a sacerdotal
institution. This object was fulfilled ; and his college
produced Wycliffe, at once one of the most eminent
of the school philosophers and the first great adver-
sary of the sacerdotal power, for the suppression of
whose doctrines, now the religion of the English
people, our earliest Academical test was imposed.

The present ascendency of the clergy, from which
the notion that the Universities are ecclesiastical institutions arises, is due to a combination of historical

accidents. The Fellows of colleges being clerks, the framers of the college statutes in the middle ages enjoined their Fellows, generally speaking, to take Holy Orders by a certain time; and as the statutes were never revised, these ordinances remained in force after the Reformation, when the real signification of taking orders had been greatly altered, and every ordained person was in fact expressly consecrated to the pastoral cure of souls *. At the same time, the colleges having grown in number and wealth, while the independent halls for students fell into decay, they absorbed the University; and thus rules and restrictions intended only for private foundations were imposed, with the clerical character which the observance of them produced, on the public institution. As a natural consequence, lay studies and professions gradually took their departure from the University; and left clerical studies, of which that of the learned languages was the chief, exclusively in possession. This result, no doubt, was partly justified in the special case of Medicine and Surgery, by the necessity of resorting to the great London hospitals; and in the special case of Pleading and Conveyancing, by the necessity of being initiated into the technical mysteries of pleaders' and convey-

---

* Persons ordained as priests are specially exhorted in the Ordination Service to give themselves to reading and learning the Scriptures, and " to forsake and put aside (as much as they may) all worldly cares and *studies.*" And they pledge themselves in the same service, " to be diligent in prayers, and in reading of the holy Scriptures, and in such studies as help to the knowledge of the same ; laying aside the study of the world and the flesh." How can men under this pledge claim the direction of secular studies, or the government of a University where such studies are pursued ?

ancers' chambers, which were to be found only in the neighbourhood of the courts of law; but in the case of all the other studies, including the studies preliminary to medicine, and the principles of jurisprudence, it was a banishment of learning and science from their natural home. Law Degrees were still required for Doctors Commons, and a premium on graduation at the University, in the shape of a remission of part of the number of law terms to be kept by the student, was formerly given at the Inns of Court; but these privileges have been recently lost, and it is to be feared that lawyers will be more than ever drawn away from the University, and that we shall become more clerical than ever, unless the increase of the number of lay fellowships, under the ordinances of the University Commission, should supply a compensating attraction. University degrees being generally, and till of late years almost universally, required by bishops as a qualification for Holy Orders, the clergy continued to graduate at Oxford and Cambridge; and by a calamitous relaxation of the University statutes respecting residence, introduced at a period of general looseness through an indiscriminate exercise of the Chancellor's dispensing power, they were enabled to proceed to the Master's degree without residing, and thus to form a Convocation of country clergymen, to whose dominion the University has long been absolutely subject. Nor was it only under the intellectual dominion of the clergy that Oxford fell: it fell also under their political dominion, and that of the political party with which they were allied. In

the time of James I. a national University became the
centre of a great conspiracy against the civil as well
as the religious liberties of the nation of which Charles
and Laud stand in history as the joint chiefs; and
this conspiracy was perpetuated, in a less noble form,
after the Revolution of 1688, by the Jacobite parsons
of Oxford common rooms, who by their intrigues,
and still more by the doctrines which they infused
into their pupils, kept alive during a century the evils
of a disputed succession, and helped to produce, though
they refrained from personally sharing, two insurrec-
tions in favour of the house of Stuart, which cost blood
more generous than their own.   Under this twofold
tyranny political as well as religious tests were formerly
imposed by the reactionary party on candidates for
degrees.   About 1622, a preacher named Knight
having thrown out some intimation that subjects
oppressed by their prince on account of religion
might defend themselves by arms, the University not
only censured him, but pronounced a solemn decree
that it is in no case lawful for subjects to make use
of force against their princes, nor to appear offensively
or defensively in the field against them.   All persons
promoted to degrees were required to subscribe to this,
and to take an oath that they not only at present
detested the opposite opinion, but would at no future
time entertain it.   "A ludicrous display," remarks
Hallam, "of the folly and despotic spirit of learned
academies."   A ludicrous and melancholy display, he
should rather have said, of the degraded state into
which learned academies fall, when, by a series of

unfortunate accidents, they are diverted from the purposes of learning, and made slaves to the clerical profession and its political allies.

Even supposing that the Universities were legally and historically the property of the national Church, the property of the national Church, as distinguished from its spiritual organisation and attributes, is the property of the nation; and the Legislature is not only entitled, but bound to deal with it, and every part of it, for the good of the whole community. But, if the foregoing view of the facts is correct, no real change of destination is required; no appropriation having taken place but by accident, and accident which carries with it nothing legally, historically, or morally entitled to any respect whatever.

A claim of right, once admitted, absolutely rules this and all political questions, leaving nothing open to debate but the mode in which the right may be best conceded and enjoyed with least detriment to the rights of others. Justice is expediency in short hand. The advantages however which would accrue to the State by the admission of all its members, without distinction of religious opinions, to the national Universities are manifest, and may be summed up in a few words; it being premised that we are speaking at present of the University, not of the Colleges, which stand on a somewhat different footing, so that their case will require some separate remarks.

This measure would bring a body of Englishmen who have now become powerful and influential, under the higher culture, which has its seat in the Universities,

and from which they have been hitherto excluded,
to the detriment of the State in which they exercise
social and political power, as well as to the detriment
of their own minds. It would restore the unity of the
nation in the matter of high education, by bringing
the youth of the upper classes, whether belonging to
the landed gentry, who are mostly Anglicans, or to the
manufacturing and commercial part of the community,
who are less within the Anglican pale, to a common
place of training, where they would imbibe common
ideas, be socially as well as intellectually fused, and
learn to understand each other: an advantage the magnitude of which any one may measure by considering how
sharp has hitherto been the social and political division
between those bred at Oxford and Cambridge and
those bred elsewhere. And further, it would enable
the Universities to become the centres of the educational system in a country where large masses of the
people, it may almost be said whole districts, are conscientious and for the most part hereditary Dissenters
from the Anglican Church, and will not give their
confidence to any institution which is administered exclusively in her interest. The expense of a University
education, both in money and time, is probably too
great to admit of our reckoning on so large an addition
as many expect to the number of the resident students, though their number will no doubt be increased
both by the removal of religious disabilities, and by the
admission of more useful and popular subjects into the
course of academical education. But there is no reason
why Oxford and Cambridge should not by their action

in the way of examining and visiting, as well as by
furnishing masters, books and other instruments of
education, exercise a most beneficial influence over the
other places of education, especially those of the different social strata, ranging from the solicitor or engineer to the small tradesman, which are embraced in
the wide term middle class. This has indeed already
been perceived by the Universities themselves, and the
idea has been acted on, though, as some think, rather
crudely and hastily, by the institution of the Middle-
Class Examinations; but religious difficulties have already been encountered, though, the examinations being
perfectly voluntary, on candidates were likely to offer
themselves whose parents or schoolmasters were very
strict Dissenters, and decidedly objected to placing education under the influence of an Anglican institution.
The late Education Commissioners, again, suggested in
their report, that the Universities should grant certifi-
cates to schoolmasters, and that they should undertake
the inspection and examination of the classical endowed
schools: and possibly it may hereafter be thought, that
if some of our sinecure Fellowships were charged with
some duties of this kind they would be not less valuable
to the holders, and more useful to the State. Supposing any central system of inspection to be desirable,
a far better, more acceptable, and more trusted centre
may be found in Universities independent of political
party than in an office connected with the executive
power. But to exercise these national functions, and
still more to be trusted with national authority to
exercise them, Oxford and Cambridge must become the

Universities of the whole nation, and it must be clearly
established, in a way in which nothing but their complete emancipation from Anglican tests will establish it,
that their proper duty is the promotion of national
learning and education, not the propagation of Anglican
opinions.

Whatever may be thought by the High Church
clergy, to whom the extirpation of Dissent always seems
not only desirable but near, a statesman, looking to the
fact that the teachers and guides of large masses of the
people are, and to all appearances must long continue
to be, Nonconformists, will think it an object that those
who exercise such an influence in the community should
be trained, by a superior education and an enlarged
intellectual intercourse, to exercise it, as far as possible,
in an enlightened and liberal way. A high Anglican
journal, and one not only very able, but very moderate
and charitable in its general tone, reviewing the other
day a book by an eminent Nonconformist, acknowledged the substantial merits of the work, but con-
cluded by remarking, as a curious fact, that 'no Dissenter could write like a gentleman.' Few things are
more irritating than to hear those who maintain an
oppressive system in their own interest taunting the
oppressed with defects which are the consequences of
the oppression. The Irish peasant, to complete the
wretchedness of his lot, is complacently pronounced a
being of degraded nature, by those whose ruthless misgovernment and wicked laws have been almost the
sole cause of his degradation. The Dissenter is held
up to derision for his want of cultivation, by those who

are all the time engaging the holders of political power
by the bribe of Church support, to exclude him, as a
social Pariah, from the institutions where alone the
highest cultivation can be obtained. The remark however, though made by those who ought to be somewhat
ashamed to make it, is not without foundation. The
writings and preachings of the Nonconformists have
been the channels of spiritual life to great masses of
the English people : they have even been almost the
sole support of religion in England at times when,
as during a great part of the last century, the
Establishment, lethargic from overendowment, filled
with unworthy ministers by family patronage, and
enslaved to the purposes of worldly politicians, lay
inert and helpless in face of spreading scepticism
and dominant vice*. But, generally speaking, they
unquestionably show, by defects of style which their
Anglican critic rather severely describes as an in-

* "In the reign of George the First," says a highly conservative
as well as a very eminent historian, "the reflecting few could perceive
that the Church of England, though pure as ever in doctrine, was
impaired in energy, and must have either help or opposition to stir
it. That impulse was in a great measure given by the Methodists.. ..
We may question now whether in virtue, in piety, in usefulness, any
Church of modern times could equal ours. Nor let any false shame
hinder us from owning, that though other causes also were at work,
it is to the Methodists that great part of the merit is due. Whilst
therefore we trace their early enthusiasm and perverted views, and
the mischief which these have undoubtedly caused, as well as the
evils of the present separation, let us never forget or deny the counter-
vailing advantage." (Lord Mahon's Hist. of England, vol. ii. p. 373, 4.)
If this be true, is the Church of England entitled to exclude Methodists
from the Universities on high grounds of religious superiority ? Can
the flame that was rekindled be so pure, the lamp at which it was
rekindled so impure ?

ability to write like a gentleman, and perhaps by
some defects deeper than those of style, that the
system of academical exclusion has not failed to produce its natural effects; and that emancipation would
be a great and certain benefit to the State, inasmuch
as it would be productive of intellectual improvement
among a body of men who, as was before said, must
be expected long to remain the guides and teachers
of a great part of the people.

The removal of sectarian antipathy will seem an
advantage only to those to whom sectarian antipathy
seems an evil, who recognise the essential unity of
the Christian character in different sects and under
different dogmatic systems, and who think it a calamity that men whose virtues are the same should
be prevented by their dogmatic differences, or rather
by the dogmatic differences of their clergy, from
heartily working together in all things for the common
good. This view of the matter, it may be said without offence, is more likely to be taken by a Christian
statesman, on whose mind the identity of the religious
character in all good men is constantly impressed by
his daily experience of dealings with men of different
creeds, than by the ecclesiastic, bound almost in honour
to maintain the close connection of practical excellence
with an exclusive system of speculative dogma, and
little disturbed probably in his theoretical allegiance
to this conviction by actual contact with the virtues of
Dissent. But to those who do take it, nothing can appear
more desirable than the mixture of members of different sects in youth, when the heart is open, when

conscientious difference of opinion is still an object
of generous respect rather than of bigoted or politic
aversion, and when personal sympathy and daily com-
panionship are likely to make short work with any
formularies, however consecrated, which stand in the
way of friendship. And if under these harmonising
influences not only sectarian antipathy should in some
measure disappear—not only men now fellow citizens in
name, should, from having been members of the same
University, become fellow citizens indeed—but the value
attached to dogma itself should decline, compared
with the value attached to a Christian character and
a Christian life, some might bewail the falling bul-
warks of the faith, but others, as we before intimated,
would hail an approach, however slight, towards the
reconciliation of the English Churches, and, more
remotely, towards the reconciliation of Christendom.

It is suggested, and even Mr. Gladstone seemed
inclined to countenance the belief, that if the Universities were thrown open to Dissenters, Churchmen
would no longer resort to them ; and that consequently,
by such a measure, the interests of the many would be
sacrificed to those of the few. The interests of the
many ought to be sacrificed to those of the few, if
the few have a right to come and the many have
no right to shut them out. No such effect however
has been produced by the admission of Dissenters as
undergraduates, even into the colleges. It has not
been produced even by the admission of Roman
Catholics, whose errors are regarded by the bulk of
the community as the most pernicious, and whose

powers of proselytism are always supposed to be such
as no truth, when brought into contact with them,
can withstand.   It has not been produced by the
removal of religious restrictions in the case of the
Universities of Scotland, though the Presbyterians of
the Scotch Establishment are as rigorously attached
to orthodoxy as the Anglicans, whether they are
equally fortunate in possessing it or not.

While people are taught by their spiritual instructors
that exclusiveness is characteristic of a Christian, and
while their exclusiveness is to be displayed only at the
cost of others, it is very likely that they will be, or
at least affect to be, exclusive : but if the question
were whether they should exclude their own children
from the benefit of a university education rather than
allow them to come into contact with fellow students
and teachers of a different communion from themselves,
it may be doubted whether a single parent would
consent to keep his son away.   Traditional bugbears
which pass for excellent arguments while the interests
of the Nonconformists only are affected, would then be
subjected to the keen scrutiny of self-interest, or the
still keener scrutiny of parental ambition.   It would
soon be discovered that there was no more danger in
listening to Faraday at Oxford, than in listening to
him in London ; and that if the sons who are in the
civil service, or in the army, who are walking the
hospital, or articled to a solicitor, may be allowed to
take their chance in a world full of heretics, without
any dereliction of religious principle on the part of
their parents, or serious danger to their own faith,

the son who is at the University might be allowed to do the same. Even the Roman Catholic clergy of Ireland, whose influence over the people is far greater than that of the clergy of the Church of England, find it impossible to restrain their flock from accepting the education offered them in government schools, or even the advantages doled out to them with a sparing and somewhat humiliating hand in the University of Dublin.

There is probably no Dissenter, perhaps no Papist, whose name has of late scattered such terror through the religious world as those of the authors of *Essays and Reviews*. Yet Rugby is overflowing, and Balliol is overflowing. You cannot find admission to either without giving several years' notice ; at Balliol not without passing an entrance examination of particular severity. People are willing enough to denounce, perhaps even to persecute : but they are not willing, nor will they ever be willing, to forego the benefit of the best education for their children.

We may be allowed, without imputing any improper motives, to think that social contempt for the Dissenters mingles in some degree with the fear of religious contagion. How many fathers would withdraw their sons from the society of men of rank of a different persuasion from their own ? How many fathers would think that the presence of such persons impaired the purity of the atmosphere in a place of education, or in any other place ? It is an easy thing to stigmatize, and exclude from the path of intellectual ambition, a methodist

preacher's son. But it is not so easy to carry the
principle which alone will justify you in doing this
consistently through all your relations with a world
in which the great and powerful are not all upon
your side *.

The greatest caution and tenderness should obviously be used in breaking up, even for the ultimate
advantage of religion itself, an existing system of
religious education : and if such would be the effect
of admitting Dissenters to the Universities, we should
be entitled, not indeed to repudiate their just claim,
but to ask for the utmost patience and forbearance
at their hands. But the truth is that, so far as the
University, as distinguished from the Colleges, is
concerned, no religious system really exists. The tests,
which are now abolished in the case of students, were
the only religious system. The discipline of the University is merely a matter of police, or at most of
ordinary morality. As a consequence of the abolition
of tests, the theological part of the University Examinations is dispensed with in the case of Dissenters.
Even when it was exacted of all, to call it part of a
religious system would have been to identify theology
with religion, whereas any crammer, or any one who
had been crammed, could have borne witness that they

---

* The argument that the admission of Dissenters to a place of
education would render it unfit for the use of the orthodox, when
employed against Mr. Bouverie's Bill, received the sanction of the
First Minister, who was rewarded for this liberal sentiment with a
chorus of liberal applause. The same statesman went rather out of
his way to show his sympathy with prize-fighting : and no one will say
that his conduct in the two cases was otherwise than consistent.

were easily separated from each other; while at Cambridge the theological element, so much prized at Oxford, was actually left out of the Examinations without producing any perceptible inferiority in the religious character of Cambridge men. Attendance at the University sermons is perhaps supposed in theory to be universal. In practice it would probably be just the same after the admission of Dissenters to degrees as it is at present.

Some persons are, it is believed, inclined to attach value to the testimony which under the system of exclusion the University is supposed to render to religious truth. Religious truth will not accept the testimony of injustice; and this testimony, if we look to facts instead of fiction, will prove to be, at bottom, that of Queen Elizabeth and her favourite the Earl of Leicester, or at best that of Archbishop Laud,— a testimony which religion need not fear to resign so long as she retains that of one simple mind or one pure heart. But the truth is, this testimony, and the 'principle' which is supposed to be involved in it, were destroyed by the Acts of Parliament which admitted Dissenters to the Bachelor's degree at Oxford, and to the Master's degree at Cambridge, without its being perceived by anybody that religion rested on a less secure foundation than before. Upon every concession which the Legislature has made during the last hundred years, by the removal of religious disabilities, to the claims of conscience and of justice, the immediate ruin of religion has been foretold, and the wrath of Heaven has been denounced against the nation if it ceased to confine all rights, honours, and emoluments to the members of a privileged Church. Those who utter these predictions must be content, like other people, to have their speculations controlled by experience. And experience, now twenty times repeated, proves that there is no truth in what they say, and that God is not a God of injustice but of justice.

It is alleged that the Dissenters themselves do not wish to come to the University, and that, if its doors were thrown open to them, they would refuse to enter; so that we are officiously pleading the cause of clients who do not desire onr advocacy. Granting' this to be the fact, the answer would be something like that which is given to those who contend that slaves ought not to be emancipated, because they are contented with their degraded lot. If the system of exclusion has rendered a number of people, and people of wealth and influence, indifferent to high culture and intellectual privileges, its operation must have been mischievous indeed. However, it remains to be seen whether it is the fact that Dissenters do not wish to come to the Universities. Are they indifferent to social position as well as to intellectual cultivation? At all events let the door be opened to them. If they come, the argument is answered. If they do not come, a grievance is removed, and no harm is done.

It is true, but few Dissenters have as yet taken advantage of the Acts of Parliament which permit them to come to the Universities as students, while they are still debarred at Oxford from taking the higher degrees, and at Cambridge from becoming members of the Senate. But though they will not come while they are thus kept on a footing of inferiority and treated as objects of legislative suspicion, it by no means follows that they will not come if they are placed on a footing of equality, and frankly admitted to the full privileges of the place. The law which excludes them from the governing body of the University is an indication, or rather an open declaration, that the institution is to be administered not impartially, but in the interests of their religious opponents. The governing bodies of the Colleges are Anglican; and, as the Masters of Private Halls must be members of Convocation, no Dissenter can open a Private Hall.

We must not be too extreme to mark the inconsistencies of those who are defending a state of things which is dear to them, but which is not easily defended, and who take up in haste whatever arguments come first to hand. We are told that it is of no use to advocate the admission of Dissenters, since they would not come to the Universities if they were permitted; and, in the same breath, we are told that they would come in with a flood, fill the governing body of the University, and commence a course of legislation hostile to the interests of the Church of England. Here, again, experience allays our fears. The House of Commons has been thrown open to "persons of divergent convictions, and persons of no conviction at all." As it represents Scotland and Ireland, as well as England, a much larger proportion of members not belonging to the Church of England has been introduced into it than would within any calculable period be introduced into the Convocation of an English University. Yet it is so far from being 'unchristianized,' or rendered hostile to Anglican interests, that a motion for inquiry into the case of the Irish Establishment, the most portentous monument of intolerance in Christendom, can scarcely obtain a respectful hearing. A legislative body, whether political or academical, drawn from the upper classes of England, will represent, probably it will only too faithfully represent, the sentiments, tone, and interests, of its class. That there may be a small minority of the other way of thinking, makes no difference in the practical result. In the case of an academical Convocation, it is peculiarly absurd to suppose that the majority would pass measures calculated not only to undermine and discredit their own religion, but to drive away from their precincts the class to their connection with which the Universities owe their position, or rather their existence. What measures of the kind can any one seriously apprehend, or even picture to himself in imagination? Convocation, when thrown open, will simply be a section of English society; and will exhibit the prevailing sentiments of that society in its character and acts. If English society ever undergoes a great change, and becomes either more mediæval and sacerdotal, or more modern and liberal, in its sentiments, than it is at present, Convocation will undergo a corresponding change. Of this each party must be prepared to take its chance; unless either party thinks itself entitled and empowered to rule the whole course of the world entirely at its own discretion. There are things of more importance to religion and to the Anglican Church than the government of the University, which nevertheless are, and must be, left with resignation to the natural current of events. We are frequently told, when a question arises concerning the Crown Professorships, that if a democratic leader, hostile to Anglicanism, should rise to power, and become First Minister, he will have the appointment of the Crown Professors. No doubt he will; and he will also have the appointment of the Bishops.

The Nonconformists will, so far as it is possible to foresee, be a very small element in the University: and common sense tells us that the smaller element is more likely to be itself absorbed and assimilated, than to absorb and assimilate the larger; especially as the larger will have the influence of wealth and rank mainly on its side. The conversion of Dissenters to the Anglican Church is little to be desired by those who have not been able to convince themselves that, in the great schism of Christendom, truth remained entire with any one of the divided Churches; and who, consequently, look less for the triumph of any one of the parts than for the reconciliation of the whole. But if conversions take place, they are more likely to be those of Dissenters to Anglicanism, than of Anglicans to Dissent. The fact is, however, that of all the dangers which beset society, this of conversion

is probably the least to be dreaded: for the number
of men in any position, who take a sufficient interest
in religion to attempt to make proselytes among those
with whom they associate, is not large: and the
number of students who take a sufficient interest in
religion to attempt to make proselytes among their
fellow students, may safely be said to be very small.
How many instances have occurred of fellow students
at the Inns of Court, fellow clerks in public offices,
officers in the same regiment, or men brought together
in any other way at the age of undergraduates, who
have converted each other? An Anglican parent might
deem himself fortunate if he could be half as sure
that his sons would not be inoculated at college with
the vice of gambling, as he might be that they would
not be inoculated with what all but the most rigid
dogmatists must allow to be the less pernicious errors
of Dissent.

If religious scepticism is abroad in English society,
it will find its way into Oxford and Cambridge, as
well as into other places. There is no help for this,
unless we think that we can suspend the Universities
in a vacuum, or carry them back by enchantment into
the middle ages: and even if we were in the middle
ages, we should find that irrational dogmatism would
always cast its shadow of doubt. The truth is, that
scepticism is already here, and in an aggravated form.
It is here because it is everywhere, both in England
and in other countries, owing to the decay of State
Creeds, which, not being true, and being no longer
upheld by sufficient power, are falling into ruin and

leaving nations, whose religious thought they have long paralyzed, weltering in perplexity and distress. It is here in an aggravated form, both in the way of positive antagonism to religion and mere disbelief, as the natural consequence of the reaction following on the great attempt to restore priestly power, and to resuscitate the religion of the middle ages, of which Oxford was recently the scene, and which again was owing to the ascendency of the clergy and the predominance of clerical objects in the University. So far from its being likely to be increased by the admission of Dissenters, it is likely to be diminished; since the Free Churches, not being fast bound by Tudor formularies, have, in spite of their too narrow sectarianism, enjoyed comparative liberty of thought, and have in some degree prepared themselves for difficulties which come upon the Established Church like a sudden avalanche, scattering confusion and dismay: besides which, the very sense of freedom is a source of assurance and tranquillity compared with the disquietude which arises among the believers in a false authority when they once begin to perceive that it is false. The evil will be still further diminished by any measure which tends to make the element of general learning and education paramount over the clerical element in the University, and thus to render us less exposed to the special convulsions and catastrophes which the clerical element is undergoing, and is likely, to all appearances, for some time to undergo.

The Protestant Nonconformists, or a part of them, have on more than one occasion disgraced themselves,

and justified, so far as any acts of theirs could justify, the conduct of their oppressors, by supporting the
fanatical members of the Established Church in the
persecution of Roman Catholics : and there seems some
reason to apprehend that an appeal made to their fears
of Popery by the advocates of exclusion might not, be
ineffective in detaching Nonconformists from the side of
University Emancipation.   There may have been some
excuse for the No-Popery cry in the times when the
Papists in England formed with those on the Continent
a great and formidable conspiracy, having the mighty
monarchies of the house of Austria for its centre,
against the civil and religious liberty of all Protestant
nations.   There can be no excuse for it now, when even
Protestant statesmen, if strongly conservative, are in
alarm lest the fall of the once great Theocracy should
be too sudden, and take the communities which have
been organized under and around it unprepared.   The
momentary appearance of reviving life which Roman
Catholicism has exhibited in this country, in the shape
of the Oxford conversions, and which has renewed our
old alarms, is due not to any return of vital energy into
the withered frame of the Roman Catholic Church
itself, but to the sacerdotal and sacramental element,
essentially Roman, which was retained in the Anglican
Church under the compromise of Elizabeth, and which
had already produced exactly the same phenomena in
the time of Laud.   How many converts have the Roman
Catholics—either the old Roman Catholics or the more
dreaded Neophytes—made, except among those who

had been led up to the verge by Tractarianism, and to whom the voice of the Roman Catholic tempter was only the echo of the resolution already formed in their own minds. Our fancy, nursed on legends of Jesuitical energy and guile, invests the most commonplace Roman Catholic not only with a zeal for his religion surpassing that of the most zealous members of other Churches, but with powers of seduction bordering on the miraculous. The Roman Catholics themselves have been led by experience to form a more modest estimate of their own gifts. At the height of the Romanizing movement at Oxford, when the most tempting opportunity appeared to offer itself to proselytizing enterprise, they kept entirely aloof from the field. No addition was made to their unpretending and unattractive little chapel in the suburbs, no eminent preacher or theologian was sent to take the place of its humble priest, not a Jesuit was ever heard of in the place. Such want of enterprise on the part of the enemy ought surely to shame the veriest coward out of his fears. It seems even that the new wine of Neophyte zeal has been very near bursting the old bottle of orthodox Romanism into which it was poured. The ' Papal Aggression' which filled the English nation with ignominious panic, had its source wholly in an element of the Anglican Establishment which the English nation persists in pressing to its bosom, while it bellows with fury at the inevitable result; which has notoriously produced exactly the same effects before, and, if preserved, will go on producing the same effects,

whenever an opening appears for a sacerdotal and sacramental reaction, so long as the Papacy, the heart of
sacerdotalism and sacramentalism, continues to exist*.
Mr. Bouverie's Bill for enabling Colleges to admit Nonconformists to fellowships was opposed in debate by an
eminent and zealous Roman Catholic, whose example,
there is reason to believe, would have been followed on
a division by other Roman Catholic members of the
House. This is a pretty plain proof that those who
best understand the interests of the Roman Catholic
Church would expect no further facilities for the propagation of their creed from the free intercourse of
students in mixed places of education. Thus much at
least of that redoubtable sagacity still lingers in its
ancient seat.

If the University were thrown open, its professorships would of course be thrown open at the same time.
This has been done in the case of the Scotch Universities without any evil consequences to religion. Ecclesiastics are in the habit of attributing to others the

---

* It would be wrong in any one to speak of these unpopular features
of the movement which bore the name, and was inspired by the genius,
of Dr. Newman, without paying the tribute due to the chivalry, disinterestedness, and greatness of its earlier days, and acknowledging that
by breaking up the 'High and Dry' regime, it did much to resuscitate
religious life among the upper classes in England. Possibly it may
prove to have done a still greater service by breaking through barriers
which would otherwise have formed a hopeless obstacle to the reconciliation of divided Churches. Nor must the spiritual experience which
its authors gained, at so great a cost to themselves, be left out of the
account in estimating the gratitude due to them, even though the
lamp kindled by their self-devotion should light the paths of others
rather than their own.

passion for proselytism which animates themselves. They imagine that if a teacher of geology or history happens not to be a member of the Anglican Church, his great aim in all his instructions will be to undermine the faith of his Anglican pupils, and that he will sacrifice to this collateral object the confidence of his audience, the interest of his science, and the scientific eminence, which so far as he has any personal end, must be his own personal end in life. Jesuitical practices are not so congenial to the natures of ordinary men. The apprehension is entirely local: nobody in London thinks it necessary to inquire whether the man of science to whose lectures he proposes to go and take his children, belongs to his own or a different communion. May it not in fact be said that lecturers on physical science especially, who are the greatest objects of suspicion, are, generally speaking, rather nervously apprehensive of giving offence in these matters and rather apt to go out of their way to conciliate the religious feelings of their hearers? As to scientific atheists, if they are to be found anywhere, as it is possible they may be in the present unhappy relations between theology and science, they are most likely to be found, not among Nonconformists, whose nonconformity can scarcely fail to be caused by some positive conviction, but among nominal professors of the State religion, burning, with a smile, a little harmless incense to the established divinity, and taking with cynical composure any tests which the established superstition may require. Besides which, it must be remembered that the real teachers of the University

are already very far from being exclusively orthodox.
Books are now our real teachers. The Professor's
chair is no longer of the importance that it was in
the middle ages as the source of new knowledge and
the organ of original thought: it has been super-
seded for these purposes by the press. Among the
list of authors recommended by the University we
find Hume and Gibbon. We find Sismondi, whose
writings are a good deal tinctured with the sentiments
of an *esprit fort*. We find Hallam, whose chapters
on ecclesiastical history contain remarks on religious
questions, especially on the Anglican doctrine of the
Eucharist, which, if delivered from a Professor's chair,
would set the University in a flame. Among the
authors not formally recommended by the University,
but in constant use and virtually acknowledged by
the examiners, is Mr. Stuart Mill, whose chapter on
Social Science embodies the atheistic theory of Comte.
Any writer, however heretical or sceptical, whose work
is likely to be of use to the students in preparing
for the examinations, is sure to find his way into
their hands. The book-shops too are open: there lie
Essays and Reviews, and the writings of Bishop
Colenso: there lie Francis Newman, Theodore Parker,
Renan, Buckle, Comte: and there will lie every other
enemy of orthodoxy whose works may be commended
to public curiosity either by their own merits or by
the denunciations of the Bishops. When conversation
turns on the religious questions of the day, it is as
free in Oxford as elsewhere, possibly it is even made
a little more free by the pleasure of breaking through

a nominal restraint. The antidotes, and in the immense majority of cases, the effectual antidotes to whatever is pernicious in these influences are the same which operate at home and which preserve men in the world åt large. No one has yet been chimerical enough to propose any other correctives. No one has suggested an Index Expurgatorius for the booksellers' shops, or even for the authors to be recognised by the University. Oxford, with her closed degrees and her open libraries and book-shops, is a city with strongly fortified gates but with no walls. The barbican and portcullis of the middle ages still frown in the tests and in the statutes enjoining Professors to 'accommodate and attemper philosophy to theology,' a worthy companion of another statute directing the clerks of the market to punish forestallers and regrators : but the adversaries of the faith, or of that self-imposed blindness which arrogates the name of faith, have free entrance at every other point.

If any tendency were really shown by Professors to abuse their chairs for the propagation of irreligion, nobody could object to the enactment of such provisions as might be requisite to put a stop to the offence. To enact statutes, or enforce that which already exists, requiring that the facts of science should be distorted by lecturers in order to adapt them to a particular creed, would be a course most undesirable on many grounds, but especially because it would manifestly bring dishonour and ridicule on religion.

The Colleges, as has been already said, stand as

regards this question on a somewhat different footing
from the University. They are private foundations;
though they hold their perpetual endowments only
by virtue of a special license of the State, which
possesses and has exercised a corresponding power of
adapting their regulations from time to time to the
requirements of the public good; and though, under
this power, most of them have been transferred from
the Roman Catholic religion, which was that of
their founders, to a religion which, as it divides the
world with the Roman Catholic Church as an antagonist, can scarcely be described with truth as her
heir. What is of more importance, it may be said
of them, while it cannot be said of the University, that
they carry on a system of religious education : a system
the efficacy of which is, indeed, preposterously over-
rated in these discussions, consisting, as it does, mainly
of compulsory attendance at chapel and at theological
lectures which leave very little religious impression
on the mind, and bearing, as it does, a very incon-
siderable proportion to home influences, and to the
spontaneous religion of Christian students ; yet one
which cannot be called altogether nugatory, or des-
titute of value in the eyes of Christian parents.
Thus the claim of the Nonconformists in the case
of the colleges is weaker than in the case of the
University, and at the same time the difficulty of
meeting it is more real. On the other hand the
fellowships are the great prizes of academical industry;
through them only can an entrance be found to that
very important part of University education which

consists in intercourse with the most intellectual
society of the place; nor can any one but the holder
of a fellowship settle down, after taking his degree,
to the pursuit of learning and science with a full
enjoyment of all appliances, and in a satisfactory
position. So that a class of students ineligible to
fellowships, though eligible to the higher degrees,
would still be in a disadvantageous and somewhat
humiliating condition.

The question is easily settled one way by those who
have made up their minds that association with any
person of a different creed from their own is dangerous,
offensive to Heaven, and almost polluting. It is
easily settled the other way by those who have made
up their minds on religious grounds, and in the interest of religion, that no difference of creed shall
ever stand in the way of their intimacy or of their
cooperation with any Christian, or, indeed, with any
honest man. But at this moment of transition and
hesitation, the minds of most men are not distinctly
made up one way or the other : and therefore it would
be difficult to say, as to the colleges generally, or as
to any particular college, how far the different ecclesiastical elements would harmonise with each other,
and whether they would unite in carrying on the
work of college education with the cordiality which
the public interest requires. It would be difficult also
to say how far this change in their religious position
would affect any special connection among the parents
of students which particular colleges may have formed,
though the fear of a general withdrawal from places

of education, otherwise in high repute, because they
were contaminated by the presence of a few Nonconformists, seems for the reasons before stated to be
absurd.   Roman Catholics are probably too much
addicted to sectarian exclusiveness to present themselves as candidates for fellowships in a mixed society.
Otherwise, there might no doubt be a difficulty in
consenting to put up with the unsocial attitude of
men who have persuaded themselves that everything
in Christendom is of the earth earthy, except that
Church which has most miserably soiled its spiritual
essence by adulterous union with the worst powers of
the earth, and by partnership, and more than partnership, in their worst crimes.

Under these circumstances there would seem on
the whole to be no better course than that proposed
by Mr. Bouverie in his Bill of last session, viz., to
repeal the clause of the Act of Uniformity requiring
Fellows of Colleges to make a declaration of Conformity
at their admission, and then to leave the Colleges free
to deal with the question by their own powers of
legislation as each of them may think fit*. This proposal received a good deal of support at Cambridge,
especially in the more distinguished colleges, and the

---

* The three colleges which availed themselves of the power given
them to amend their own statutes during the first year of the late
Parliamentary Commission have the power of amending all their
statutes for the future, with the consent of the Visitor. The rest, for
which, the first year having expired, the Commission made ordinances
by default, have the power of amending those ordinances with the
consent of Her Majesty in Council, and the rest of their statutes with
the consent of the Visitor.

petition sent up against it from Oxford was opposed by fifty-one members of Convocation, whose votes, it will not be very rash to say, were a better indication of the interest of the University as a place of learning and education, and of the interest of the community at large as distinguished from that of an ecclesiastical party, than the 180 votes given on the other side. It is true that the measure was discouraged, and in effect quashed by the present leader of the Liberal party, which proves, no doubt, that it was sincerely liberal in its character, but is very far from proving that it was injudicious or extreme.

The Oxford colleges in elections to fellowships are bound, under their new Parliamentary Ordinances, to choose that candidate, who, after examination, shall be found to be " of the greatest merit and most fit to be a fellow of the college as a place of religion, learning, and education." And their duty to education as well as to religion would require them under these words to reject every candidate who had shown by his previous conduct that he was likely to set an example of profanity or levity, to abuse his influence as a fellow for the purpose of proselytism among the students, or otherwise to give just offence and bring discredit on the society in matters of religion. On the other hand, they would not be bound or authorised, nor are they bound or authorised now, to give any weight to mere party sympathies or antipathies, to entertain vague suspicions suggested by loose tongues, or to institute an inquisitorial scrutiny into the

thoughts of men, over whose faith, in a time of
general controversy and perplexity, a cloud may perhaps
be passing, but whose character may not, perhaps, be
on that account less essentially religious, nor their presence in a community less acceptable to really religious
men.   That those who have themselves been the great
disturbers of men's minds in these matters, who have
themselves introduced before our eyes, under the name
of a revival, a new religion, the doctrines and ritual
of which are still unsettled and in course of furtive
development; who have led away many of the youth
of England from the paths in which their fathers had
walked for generations, and landed not a few of them
in Roman Catholicism, and some in blank unbelief—
that such men above all others should be extreme
to mark and punish disturbance of conscience and
unsettlement of faith, would not perhaps be very
surprising, but it would be most ungenerous and
unjust.   And surely if to win waverers back to
Christianity were the end in view, odious imputations
and harsh treatment — harsh treatment at the age
when it is most deeply felt and makes the most lasting impression—would not be the best means to that
end.   What is right rather than what is politic, should
be the question when religion is concerned : but if policy
is to be considered at all, it should be remembered
that no enemies of religion are likely to be more deadly
or more dangerous, than those who have felt religious
injustice in their youth.

    A large proportion of the Fellows in all the colleges,
except All Souls, and the Heads of every college except

Merton, must be in Holy Orders*. This is a very strong guarantee against any disturbance of the religious system of college education; and a still stronger guarantee will probably be found, so long as the sentiments of English society remain what they now are, in the influence of public opinion. With regard to education, indeed, the admission of Nonconformists as undergraduates, which has already taken place in a few instances, might have been thought more subversive of the existing system, the rules of which it is necessary to break through in these cases, than the admission of Nonconformist Fellows, who would not necessarily take any part whatever in the college education. The Act of Parliament requiring the Service of the Church of England to be performed daily in the college chapel would of course remain unaffected by any change in the Statutes respecting the election of fellows : and as the college is not the Ordinary, no majority of the fellows, supposing them to be so strangely inclined, would have the power of interfering with the college worship in any way whatever. So that those who look not to mere names and professions, often dignified with the title of principles, but to substantial results, might feel sufficiently secured against the destruction of anything which could possess a real value in their eyes. Whatever change did take place, moreover, would take place very gradually, and almost imperceptibly. Many years would probably elapse before Nonconformists would

* The Head of Oriel may by the Statutes be a layman, but a great part of the income consists of a canonry of Rochester annexed to the Provostship.

F

offer themselves in any considerable numbers as candidates for fellowships, and by that time it is quite possible that the hostile relations between those who are now distinguished as Churchmen and those who are now distinguished as Nonconformists may have undergone some change. The first effect of the relaxation would be to admit to fellowships men who have no desire to separate themselves practically from the Church of England, but whose consciences refuse, on moral and religious grounds, to take any kind of religious test. Cases of this kind have, it is believed, already occurred : and they involve peculiar hardship and absurdity, because the man who refuses on such grounds to become, like his contemporaries, a candidate for a fellowship, is driven to place himself before the University in the position of a Nonconformist, or even of a disbeliever in Christianity, when in point of fact he may be perfectly willing to remain in the Church in which he has been worshipping, and may object to nothing but the test. Even a Nonconformist, in the full sense of the term, though he might be honourably reluctant to renounce, for the sake of a fellowship, the communion of his fathers, would probably, in nine cases out of ten, after passing through the training of the University, and mingling for several years in its society, be very far from a separatist in temper or in practical religion. The Scotch and English Establishments, so far as the mass of their members are concerned, are in practical communion with each other, the Supreme Head of the English Establishment herself attending public worship according to the form of the Scotch Establishment when she is in that part of her dominions : and nothing can be more irrational than to exact of a Scotch candidate for an English fellowship an act of ostensible apostasy, which to him is corrupting and humiliating, while to us it is valueless, or rather unmeaning. In effect, the religious character of the colleges would take its complexion from that of society at large; a result of which the members of a free community would scarcely have reason to complain. But unluckily there are many men who have not thoroughly learned to regard themselves as members of a free community, or to think that the wishes of society at large are entitled to respect, but who still act on the assumption that they are members of a dominant party and sect, to which all national privileges exclusively belong, while the rest of the nation are in the position of suppliants and mendicants, whose importunities must be stoutly resisted at once, lest they should be emboldened in the end to demand a full measure of justice.

It would be uncandid to deny that the Colleges would have difficulties and perhaps some internal dissensions to encounter, in the transition from one system to the other. The difficulties would probably be greatly diminished if the mere prize fellowships, tenable by non-residents as sinecures, could be separated from those held by the tutors of the college ; a measure which is most desirable, and indeed will probably soon be found absolutely necessary, in order to secure to colleges a sufficient number of resident teachers in the different departments. But whatever they may

be, we have to set against them the gathering danger
of a system of exclusion, which arrays against us not
only the professed Nonconformist, but the able men
of independent minds, who, their consciences being
awakened, will no longer submit to the degradation
of taking anything in the nature of a test. As to
the dissension among the Fellows, it would scarcely
be greater than that caused by the difference of
opinion which prevailed in almost every college on
the subject of the recent reforms, and which, it may
confidently be said, has left behind no feelings of
bitterness comparable to those which are frequently
engendered by the election of a Head.

It is very probable that colleges would take different courses in this matter, according to their different tempers and connections. If they did, the
anomaly would not be very startling, considering the
mass of anomalies, ecclesiastical and political, by which
we are surrounded; and the arrangement would probably be one fairly adapted, in a practical point of
view, to the exigencies of the case. The Church of
England, in fact, comprehends in herself, beneath the
ostensible unity of the Establishment, a number of
different sects, ' High Church,' ' Low Church,' and
' Broad Church,' which are at variance with each other,
not only on secondary points of doctrine, but as to the
very channels of spiritual life. Some of these sects
demand greater exclusiveness than others. Some are
much farther removed than others from the Evangelical portion of the Nonconformists. The independent action of the several colleges on this question

would probably provide for each sect colleges suited to its religious needs. And if there are any who prefer comprehension, and think the air of freedom favourable to religion, they are surely entitled to consideration among the rest.

It is convenient to have before us the objections to a proposed measure, in a compendious and authoritative form. The objections to repealing the clause of the Act of Uniformity, which requires persons elected to fellowships to make a declaration of Conformity, and thus setting the colleges free to legislate for themselves in the matter, as here proposed, are set forth compendiously, and with the highest authority, in the Petition of the University against Mr. Bouverie's Bill; which was afterwards printed as a manifesto, and signed by the Archbishops of Canterbury and York, six Bishops, several lay Peers, and a very large proportion of the non-resident Members of Convocation. An examination of this document will, it is believed, tend to convince any statesman who looks at the question in the interest of the whole community, and not merely in that of an ecclesiastical party, that the objections, compared with the advantages, are not of very great weight.

The adverse authority of so many ecclesiastics of the highest rank is no doubt expected to daunt the advocates of reform. Yet the same adverse authority has been encountered by every reformer in turn; even by those whose reforms, as all men of sense now perceive, did the most essential service to religion by redeeming her from the taint of injustice and reconciling her to the moral sense of an alienated nation. It is no flourish of rhetoric, but the simple and sober truth, to say that if no measure had been carried of which the Bishops did not approve, the country would have been long since plunged into revolution : and Catholic Emancipation was in fact resisted at their instigation till the Duke of Wellington recoiled from the verge of civil war. Placed as these Prelates are, difficult of defence as their own political position is, they would show not only a disinterestedness, but a freedom from the spirit of their order more than human, if they were not habitually averse to change : and when their titles are set in array against us, we may reasonably ask to have their bias as well as their rank taken into the account. As to the University Convocation, from which, in the first instance, the document emanates, it is, as has been said before, a mere organ of the clerical profession, which has compelled a learned and scientific institution, or rather the body of such an institution possessed by an alien spirit, to appear before the Legislature as the opponent of almost every great measure of progress, including Railways as well as Catholic Emancipation.

The mass of those who signed with the Archbishops and Bishops were, as might have been expected, clergymen, of whose professional bias in these matters no one can be ignorant, and whose interests, it cannot be too often repeated, are those of an order, though a most important order, not those of the whole nation. Neither the number of the objectors therefore, nor the rank of some of them, can be held to absolve the Legislature in the present case from scrutinising their reasons.

Those reasons are comprised in three clauses. The first clause sets forth, "That the removal of the only test now by law required of tutors and fellows of colleges generally would render admissible to collegiate government and instruction persons of divergent religious creeds, or of no religious creed whatever." It is not to be denied that the removal of a religious restriction will render admissible persons who were before excluded on account of religion : such was not only the obvious tendency but the avowed object of Mr. Bouverie's Bill. But the question submitted to the judgment of statesmen is, what will be the practical effect of the relaxation? Will the character of college government and instruction be really rendered less religious? Are any other practical evils likely to result comparable in magnitude to the advantage of relieving conscience and opening these great places of education to the whole community? Will not religion, on a broad and statesmanlike view of its interests, be the gainer by this as it has been by other measures of emancipation? 'Persons of no religious creed' is a customary phrase when these alarms are to be raised. But what is its exact meaning? If it means profane scoffers at religion, it will remain the duty of the electors under their general trust, as guardians of a place of "Religion, Learning, and Education," to exclude such persons, notwithstanding the removal of the test. If it means persons labouring under sincere doubt and disturbance of conscience on

religious subjects, it may very well be questioned
whether contact with such persons ever made an
irreligious impression, or failed to make something
of a religious impression on any man or society. In
fact, as has been said before, such persons are already
to be found among the fellows of colleges; yet the
mischievous effects of their presence had not become
visible to the framers of the petition, who assume
that, at present, all is well. There is indeed another
class of persons 'of no religious creed whatever,' in
any deep sense of the term, whose presence and example
may teach young hearts to mistrust religion : but these
persons are likely to be found, not bending under the
burden of obloquy which a world at once careless and
pharisaical casts on honest doubt, but nimbly mounting
the ladder of preferment, and denouncing, from the high
places of the Church, for the gratification of the religious public, men who have braved everything and
sacrificed everything for the sake of religious truth.

The next clause is, "That the Universities are
seminaries of the Church of England, and owe their
greatness chiefly to their connection with the Church ;
and that the Church could not safely entrust her
future clergy to persons who had given no security
for their soundness in the faith." The first part of
this rather complex and not very coherent proposition
has been, in effect, answered before. It is not true,
legally or historically, that Oxford and Cambridge
are "seminaries of the Church of England." They
are legally lay corporations : historically they are
national Universities, which in their most memorable

era were rather antagonists than servants of the clergy; but in which clerical influence has since, through a combination of accidents, become supreme. That the University owes its greatness to its connection with the Church is, in one sense, most true. These, like all the other institutions of Christendom, owe, and will continue to owe, their greatness to the spirit of Christianity, which, regardless of the barriers erected between one Christian community and another by clerical schisms and state creeds, still pervades and secretly unites the divided frame, everywhere sustaining self-devotion, the source of greatness; and which perhaps has often been present, though uninvoked, at the beneficent labours of the study and the laboratory, while it has been absent, though invoked, from the formal rites of an intolerant and cruel state religion. The presence among us of a large proportion of students and men of learning devoted to a spiritual calling is also of inestimable value, provided that they will be content to use the University and exert their due influence in it without making it their slave. But no one, without setting at defiance the plainest facts of academical history, can pretend that this University, as a seat of learning and science, has been greatest when it has been most under the dominion of the clergy. It was greatest, as has been said already, in the thirteenth and fourteenth centuries, when it was the centre of mental activity in all departments, and really led the intellect of the nation. It was least great, or rather it was most degraded, in the eighteenth century, when it was absolutely in the hands of the clergy and of the High

Church party among the clergy, and when learning and science were almost exiles from its walls, education sank into a farce, the professorial chairs were silent, and so much of the time of the Heads and Fellows as was not consumed in 'deep but dull potations,' was spent in fomenting High Church conspiracies against the peace and liberty of the nation. Even Theology has failed to profit in any way by the efforts of a clerical legislature to put every other subject of study under her feet: and monopoly in this case, as in others, has proved most injurious to the monopolists themselves.

If the University has recently revived, and become more useful and an object of greater respect to the nation; if great reforms have been made, our revenues more fairly distributed, and our fellowships and scholarships opened to merit; if physical science, jurisprudence, and political economy have been recalled, or are being recalled, from their long banishment, and the chairs of their teachers are being properly endowed; all this has been done notoriously under the pressure of public opinion, notwithstanding the opposition of the clerical party, as represented by its most influential leaders, though, it must be gratefully acknowledged, with the aid and under the guidance of some members of the order, among the highest in intellect, and, if to engage the confidence of cultivated and independent minds is a service, not among the lowest in their services to religion.

As a seat of science especially the University seems as far as possible from owing any greatness she may possess to clerical dominion, particularly at the present crisis. An antagonism has evidently arisen between science and theology, the source of which lies not in the nature of the subjects themselves (for it would be absurd to suppose that truth could be the antagonist of truth) but in the difference of the modes in which they have respectively been studied. Science has been studied at once freely and with humility, by that method of patient and conscientious investigation which, for purposes obviously connected with our moral training, the Creator has prescribed as the sure and the only road to truth. Theology has been studied neither freely nor with humility, but dogmatically, that is at once slavishly and arrogantly, in a way that never has led, nor, till the ordinances of the Author of Truth are changed, ever will lead, to the attainment of the truth. The natural consequence is, that while science has rapidly advanced and obtained a great and too engrossing dominion over the mind of man, theology has fallen into decay : it has fallen into decay so completely, that philosophers of a certain school are beginning, not without plausibility or without success, to represent it as merely a transitory and now extinct mode of explaining phenomena, of which science offers the true and final explanation. This state of things will doubtless be reversed so soon as theology begins to be studied by as sound a method as science ; and science will then lower its pretensions to their proper level and recede into its own domain. But in the meantime it is not to be expected that the two studies should be very good friends to each other, or that their votaries should be free from mutual suspicion. Not that men of science are, as a class, irreligious. As a class they are probably far less irreligious than ordinary men of the world, even those men of the world in whom clerical confidence is most reposed; nor do they, generally speaking, show any tendency to renounce Christianity, or to separate themselves in life or death from the communion of Christendom. They are in fact still held in allegiance by those substantial and rational truths of Christianity which barren and irrational dogma only overlays. But they would be sinners against the light that is in them if they did not recoil from mere absurdities, particularly when tendered in a damnatory form and stamped as falsehoods to all uncorrupted minds by their connection with a spirit of persecution. Hence the existence of science in the University of Oxford is a hard struggle against theological jealousy, which sometimes breaks forth in rather animated expressions. The motives of the theological party are such as ought not for a moment to be impugned. They are contending for what they rightly think a higher object against an object which they rightly think lower, though it is to be hoped that they are wrong in thinking the two incompatible. But there can be little doubt that if their wishes had prevailed science would scarcely have been re-admitted into the University: and there can be as little doubt that if their wishes could now prevail, it would either be banished once more or studied and taught under such conditions as would render it the scorn of the intellectual world. Such a result would be peculiarly adverse to the greatness of the University at a moment when science, owing to its recent achievements, and still more to the ground of certainty which its conclusions afford amidst the apparent uncertainty and inconclusiveness of theology and philosophy, enjoys an exceptional degree of reverence, so that, without it, no intellectual institution can command the confidence of men.

The latter part of the clause last quoted asserts, "That the Church could not safely entrust her future clergy to persons who had given no security for their soundness in the faith." We will not here discuss the assumption that tests, so often taken with a smile by open unbelievers, are securities for soundness in the faith. But we must ask what assurance the Oxford Council who framed this document, or even the Prelates and others who afterwards signed it, can have of their own competency thus to speak for the national Church. The national Church legally speaking is the English nation : while the practical arbiters of clerical education are the holders of Church patronage, who form the "congregation" by which "ministers" are "lawfully called" to their office in an establishment. And it may be pretty confidently predicted that the nation at large, and the holders of patronage if they shared the general sentiments of their countrymen, would continue to prefer clergymen trained in a place of free education, even though it might contain some Dissenters, to clergymen trained in an exclusive "seminary" under teachers of their own order. Reaction has not gone so far as to make the English people forget their dislike of priests and Jesuits, or of spiritual guides trained in a priestly and Jesuitical school. Nor does there seem any reason to believe that the mass of men intending to become clergymen would differ in their feelings on this point from their countrymen generally; or that they would be wanting in the contemptuous repugnance felt by almost all Englishmen to things which seek seclusion from light and air. If the University continued to give the best education and to bestow on those trained in her schools the means of intellectual influence over the people, she would, in all probability, continue to attract students destined for the clerical calling: and neither she nor they would suffer a deprivation which to her, as has been admitted, would be very great, and which would be at least equally great to them. Something they might lose perhaps in corporate zeal; but they would gain more in individual power. Something they might lose as champions of orthodoxy; but they would gain more as teachers of the truth. And when we consider to what moral liabilities men destined for the cure of souls are already exposed in the course of their undergraduate life, and the complacency with which the beneficial effects of freedom are accepted as a full compensation for a mass of moral evils, it is difficult to forbear smiling at the fears of those who regard with so much horror the additional danger of a somewhat earlier contact with differences of religion, of the existence of which the student is of course perfectly aware. Why is the daily and hourly sight of Nonconformity at home and in the world harmless, but at the University ruinous to faith?

The third objection is, " That the relations between fellows of colleges are very intimate, and that the harmony and confidence now subsisting must be destroyed by differences on the most important of all subjects." When we consider that these words are penned by men who have the facts before their eyes, and countersigned by men in high and responsible stations, who had the facts before their eyes but yesterday, and when we also consider that the statement is made for a purpose affecting the rights of others, some thoughts arise in the mind to which on the whole it is better not to give expression. If the harmony and confidence subsisting between fellows of colleges have not been disturbed by the violent controversies and mutual persecutions of the last thirty years, they must be tolerably proof against disturbing influences of that kind; and we may justly as well as charitably infer that the fellows are not so wanting in Christian courtesy, or so despicably incapable of living on good terms with those who conscientiously differ from them in matters of religion, as the authors of this manifesto would make them out to be.

We have spoken of religious education in the colleges, and admitted that on that special point there might be fair ground for apprehending a difficulty, which, however, would in practice probably soon melt away. There is no other relation between fellows of colleges, nor is anything else transacted between them, as the framers and supporters of the University Petition are very well aware, with which, if the fellows are men of common sense and common good breeding, a difference of religious opinion need in any way interfere. Many of the fellows, a large majority of them indeed, are habitually non-resident, and merely draw their income. And no man, if his own rights and interests were in question, not those of others, would pretend that he could not dine in the hall, drink his wine and read the newspaper in the common room, or take part in college meetings for the management of the estates with men of a different way of thinking from himself about the order of Bishops or the Athanasian Creed. We all do this every day of our lives.

That mutual persecution is subversive of harmony and confidence, and of the efficiency to which harmony and confidence are indispensable, may be readily admitted. But the mutual persecution which now rages has its sole source and sanction in the Tests, and must cease at once when they are removed.

The fourth and last objection, which is rather incongruously blended into one clause with the third, is " That open antagonism in the religious belief of their teachers and governors must have a tendency to lead students to regard religious truth as a matter of indifference." One should have supposed that antagonism (if it must be so called) in the religious belief of conscientious men would rather have a tendency to lead students (if students have any sense) to regard religious truth as a matter of great importance to both the contending parties. Suppose the framers of this document had been present when St. Paul withstood St. Peter to the face, would they have inferred that neither of the two Apostles cared

anything for Christianity? What they probably
mean is that we should no longer be able to point
to the exclusive enjoyment of academical emoluments by the professors of the true religion, as an
evidence of its truth: but probably this evidence is
less cogent, and the withdrawal of it would be less
fatal, in the eyes of students, still in the season of
enthusiasm and disinterestedness, than in the eyes of
older and shrewder men. It will be observed, too,
that it is *open* antagonism alone which the petitioners
deprecate. *Real* antagonism, and that on the most
vital questions, they know already exists among us;
but they think that a nominal unity is still valuable,
though sincere unity is notoriously gone. In whose
eyes is a nominal unity valuable? In those of sensible
men, or in those of the allseeing God?

A collection of hymns, made by a very eminent
member of this University, and one whose name is
greatly respected by the High Church party, is now
in every one's hands. These hymns, like all good
hymns, express the very deepest feelings of religion;
feelings, to be united in which, is to be united in
the very essence of spiritual life. Many of those in
the collection are the work of professed Nonconformists. Others are the work of men of the extreme
Evangelical party, who were regarded as virtual Nonconformists, though they were nominally within the
pale of the Established Church. And we are told
that the men whose most fervent outpourings of
devotion are here mingled together could not, without scandal and disparagement to Christianity, have

G

performed the common offices of life together. We
are told that Heber and Charles Wesley could not
have lived peaceably within the same college walls';
or that, if they had, the students would have been
led to regard religious truth as a matter of indifference!
Who would write such things anywhere but in a
University petition?

Sectarianism in the eyes of sectarians is fidelity to
principle: in the eyes of statesmen it is an evil.
Every statesman, looking to the calamities of all kinds
which have flowed directly or indirectly from the
religious divisions of England and of Christendom,
must desire that these divisions shall, if possible, be
brought to an end. It is vain to hope that the
reunion will be effected by controversies on questions
of dogma which have been carried on without an
approach to agreement for centuries, and may be
carried on with the same absence of result for ever;
the questions being, in fact, such as reason can
never determine, and at the same time perfectly
unpractical, so that neither party can have any practical motive for giving up that which each has been
trained, as a point of ecclesiastical honour, and as
an article of salvation, obstinately and even blindly
to maintain*. It will be effected, if at all, and has

---

* Who, for example, can hope that the Clergy of the Western
Churches will convert those of the Eastern, or that those of the Eastern
will convert those of the Western, by controversial reasoning on the
question respecting the "Procession" of the Third Person from the
Second Person of the Trinity ; a doctrine to which no human understanding can attach any meaning whatever, and which, therefore, no
argument can touch, while the opposite dogmas are rooted in the minds

to some extent already been effected, by measures of
political and social emancipation, which throw men of
different sects together in the offices of political and
social life, and make them sensible of each other's
virtues, whereby Christian morality, the uniting
element, is brought by degrees into the foreground,
and dogma, the dividing element, is by degrees
thrown into the background, and may, in the end
pass practically out of view. This consideration, as
well as those of mere political justice and tranquillity,
will, in the eyes of statesmen, be an inducement to
embrace a policy of emancipation. But it will be
the reverse of an inducement in the eyes of those to
whom theoretically, if not practically, dogma is the
essence of religion.

The only further observation to be made on the
University petition, against the emancipation of the
Colleges, is that it evidently emanates from persons
who regard the preservation of "the last test" as a
matter on which the life of the Church depends;
whereas, many public men must by this time have made
up their minds, that the last test is the last leaf
upon the bough, which will hang only till the winds
awake, and that the religion of the nation must
henceforth be founded, and is capable of being founded,
on the broader and more enduring basis of social
equality and justice.

One more point remains, which shall be mentioned

of the combatants by pride, habit, and the traditional conviction that
the repetition of the affirmative, or of the negative form of words, is
essential to salvation ?

separately, as it lies beyond the scope both of the Petition against Religious Tests and of Mr. Bouverie's Bill. It is commonly proposed by the advocates of University emancipation, as a reasonable compromise with the other party, to open the Faculties of Arts, Law, and Medicine, but to leave the theological Faculty confined to the Established Church; and the principle of this proposal was followed in the Cambridge University Act, which excepted the Theological Degrees from the general measure of relaxation. The friends of liberal measures are perhaps rather too ready to sacrifice anything connected with the department of theology, which they have had too much reason to think utterly hopeless, as a propitiation to their opponents. Looking at the question however as we are here endeavouring to look at it, in the interest of the whole community, there seems some reason to believe than an open Faculty of Theology might at the present moment be the most important of all.

It must be evident to every man, and almost to every child, that religious doubt has overspread the face of Christendom. This is not the place to inquire what limits would be assigned to the extent of the calamity by an observer capable of taking a calm and comprehensive view of the religious world in all its parts, and of distinguishing the mere disintegration of Byzantine and Roman dogma, or the final decay of the mediæval Theocracy, from the actual growth of convictions opposed to the fundamental and vital truths of Christianity as set forth in the New Testament, which really sustain Christian society and life. No new religion, or substitute for a new religion, has yet appeared, except the bastard Christianity of Rousseau and the crazy worship of Humanity which emanated from the decaying reason of Comte : nor do men who have manifestly rejected the dogmatic creeds of Christianity and a great part of its historical evidences cease to bring up their children as Christians, or visibly to draw their own spiritual life from Christian influences acting on them through the community in which they live. Here, however, it is enough to say, what we all perceive and most lament, that doubt is now in the hearts and on the lips of men ; that it not only finds vent in a great body of sceptical writings on theology, which are the more eagerly read the more anxiously they are discountenanced by the clergy, but pervades, in a more subtle but not less seductive shape, the works of the popular philosophers, historians, poets, and novelists, by whom the sentiments of the age are at once expressed and formed ; that it begins to exercise a disturbing influence even on the moral convictions of society ; that it paralyzes or perplexes social as well as individual action, and enfeebles the characters of leading men, to whom society looks in vain for the cure of its maladies when they are unable to heal their own ; and that it fills all men and nations with perplexity and with deep mistrust of the future. It may probably be said that at the present time, as in the sixteenth century, the restless heavings and tossings of society, which on a superficial view appear to be merely political revolutions, are in part at least the outward symptoms of the deeper disturbance which fills the soul of the world,

and of which every educated man, if he will speak the
truth to himself, will acknowledge the presence in his
own heart. This state of things must be a matter of
anxiety to the statesman as well as to the theologian.
For that religion is the basis of civilization, the only
sufficient sanction of the moral principles on which
society depends, and the only lasting spring of the
unselfish affections and actions which bind men into
a community, and save that community from disso-
lution, is admitted by all philosophic observers of real
eminence, even by those who adore God under the
disguise of Nature, or who pay religious worship to
scientific facts, dignified, by a transparent misnomer,
with the title of laws. A prolonged period of scepticism therefore cannot fail to produce social and political disaster, the evils of which the continued existence
of a state religion, when once generally felt to be
untrue, will aggravate, both by inflaming the destructive
violence of scepticism, and by preventing the free action
of the reconstructive power.

The French Revolution, though it has been graphi-
cally described by more than one great historian, has
never been thoroughly analyzed as a political phe-
nomenon for the purposes of political science. But
we can have little hesitation in pronouncing which of
its complex causes was the deepest and most powerful.
De Tocqueville's work on the *Ancien Régime*, among
others, has shown that the misgovernment, though
great, was not great enough to produce so terrible a
convulsion. The economical distress prevailed most in

the rural districts, which were not the chief seat of the revolution. And the subsequent history of France, indeed that of the revolutionary government itself, proves that there was not in the French people a deeply seated hatred of monarchy, or a strong desire for a republic. Rousseauism, embodied in the Jacobins, proved itself the strongest element in the struggle, as extreme Puritanism, embodied in Cromwell and the Independents, proved itself the strongest element in the English Revolution : and the deepest cause of the catastrophe was the religious disturbance, of which Voltaire represented the more critical, Rousseau the more emotional, and therefore the more energetic part. A State religion had been maintained by a despotic government in a very hateful and oppressive form, long after it had ceased to command the intellectual allegiance of the more educated and active-minded part of the people : a prolonged period of covert scepticism masked by an outward conformity ensued, the Court itself ceasing to feel, or even to pretend, respect for the State Church which it supported; until, the pressure of economical distress and a crisis of political difficulty coinciding with a convulsive effort to attain to a new religious, or at least a new social, faith, the whole of the undermined surface gave way, and brought temple and tower together in ruin to the ground. The State religion has not been so exclusively enforced, nor has the yoke of the State clergy been so heavy in this country as in France before the revolution : the mischief done to the faith of the nation has therefore not been so great: but nevertheless great mischief has been done, and statesmen will soon be called upon to deal with the results.

To put the same thing in another way, the account of the present distress is to be sought in the long suspension of religious thought, and the consequent accumulation of religious difficulties pressing for solution. It is no disparagement to Christianity, as the sole and sufficient source of spiritual life, to say that its advent did not consign the religious intellect of man to perpetual torpor, or condemn it for ever to the scarcely intellectual function of handing down and repeating certain theological formularies, drawn up in the primitive or early ages of the Church. The general plan of the Creator's dealings with us would lead us, on the contrary, to expect that active service would be required of the intellect in matters of religion as well as in other matters: and that difficulties and problems would be, from time to time, presented to us in religion, in the effort to solve which man would deepen his religious character, and see farther into the things of God. Not but that there was a faith which was committed to the Church by its Founder, to be simply held for ever, and which those who sold the spiritual independence of the Church for State endowments, and the support of political power, most miserably, and almost to the ruin of Christendom, betrayed. If however such is the arrangement of Providence, it is plain that the religious intellect of man cannot with impunity be kept in forced inaction, while all other kinds of speculation and knowledge continue to ad-

vance. Yet it is this that the old governments of
Europe, moved partly by bigotry, partly by fear, and
prompted by the holders of Church endowments, have
done by means of their State Churches; which have
suspended religious thought, so far as it could be suspended, by perpetuating, in Roman Catholic countries,
the superstition of the middle ages; and in Protestant
countries, by arresting the movement of the Reformation at different points, all equally arbitrary, and deter-
mined not by reason or conscience, but by political
power. That which these politicians have so long been
sowing, we have now reaped. And if the cause of the
malady be here rightly assigned, the cure is to set the
religious intellect free, and allow it to grapple, though
late, with the difficulties which, through its previous
inaction, coupled with the activity of science, have
gathered round the faith of Christendom.

The priest party on the Continent, of course, sum-
marily explain the spread of religious doubt as a gra-
tuitous outbreak of human wickedness; and proceed
to allay it by darkening, as far as they can, the pec-
cant reason of all under their influence, by bringing
into play the machinery of religious terror, and by
tendering the alliance of the Church to political rulers,
even the most notorious debauchees and atheists, as
the price of measures of ecclesiastical reaction. A
similar view of the case is taken, and an analogous
course is pursued, by the corresponding party in this
country, who, in the time of need, are almost as little
fastidious as their brethren on the Continent in scru-
tinizing the religious character of those whom they

deem useful as political allies. Those who think more
charitably of human nature, and who believe that
human reason is the work of God, will remark that
though prolonged scepticism unquestionably has a tendency to shake the foundations of morality, many of
those whose hearts are filled with religious doubt are
among the best of men, the purest in life, the most
disinterested in their objects, the most ready to sacrifice everything to truth and right; and generally, that
this age, though perplexed in religious belief, is on
the whole not much inferior to any of those that have
gone before in heroism and self-devotion, however
readily priests may account for these qualities, when
displayed on the wrong side, as cunning delusions of
devils counterfeiting the appearance of angels of light.
They will further observe, that scepticism is most
prevalent in those countries where the previous repression of religious inquiry has been most severe :
and notably, that under the immediate pressure of the
Papacy and of the great Catholic despotisms which
were its instruments of coercion, the extinction of faith
has been almost entire.   And thus they will rather
be led to conclude, both on grounds of moral justice
and of policy, that the right mode of dealing with
the malady is, not to adopt measures of repression
(which in truth it might on many grounds be difficult to carry into effect with sufficient force), but to
give men, if possible, new assurance of their faith.

    And how is this new assurance of faith to be given?
Every man knows in his heart that it can be given only
by free, patient, and careful inquiry, carried on with

the requisite knowledge, and with a single-hearted love
of truth. If there is a God, and if His voice speaking
in our nature does not mock us, we shall be led to
the truth in this and in no other way. But who is to
carry on the free inquiry? Not the theologians of the
Established Church, for they are precluded by law from
seeking truth on the questions as to which doubt has
arisen, and bound under the severest penalties to
maintain the very doctrines which are called in
question, notwithstanding any new arguments which
may be brought forward, and any new facts which
the progress of learning and science may disclose.
That the function of an Established Clergy is to teach,
not truth, but the doctrines prescribed by the State,
and that, in fact, the business of such a clergy is not
with truth, is laid down by Sir Stephen Lushington,
in his memorable judgment, with an unflinching breadth
of statement which reminds us of the terrible decision
of Judge Ruffin on the condition of the Slave. "It
is said this authoritative imposition of doctrine would
deny to clergymen participation in modern discoveries
of science or history. A difficulty thus arises. On the
one hand it seems not reasonable to suppose that it
was intended to shut out all inquiry and abnegate all
future discoveries, however important. On the other,
the Act of the Legislature proceeded on this basis, that
for the purposes intended, the Church was in possession
of all the truth, and that nothing in that respect
remained to be discovered. Accordingly the Articles
were framed, and all clergymen forbidden under severe
penalties to impugn them. But, to remove all doubt,

I will put the case in a strong point of view. I will
presume a discovery to be made of great importance,
and proved to the satisfaction of very many scholars
and divines, and that such discovery militates against
some of the Articles. What is the duty of a clergyman? what of the Court? Is the clergyman at liberty
to use such discoveries so as advisedly to maintain what
is repugnant to the Articles? I apprehend, certainly
not. *Is the Court to discuss whether the discovery be a
real or true discovery, to define its effect and operation?
The Court can do no such thing; it has only to administer
the law. The duty of the Court is to shut its ears to all
such discoveries. It is bound by law so to do. The law
must be obeyed even in what may be termed most extra-
vagant circumstances.* The Court of Queen's Bench pro-
claimed and adhered to that principle in the case of
Ashford *v.* Thornton (1. B. and Ald. 460), where Wager
of Battel was demanded. Assuming the possibility of
such discoveries as I have supposed, *the consequence
may arise that discussions by the clergy, leading to truth,
may be excluded:* but if such indeed be the case, and
if it should be deemed to need redress, recourse must
be had to the highest authorities, viz. the Legislature,
which established the Articles and Book of Common
Prayer." Even the Bible is a sealed book to the
theologian of the Established Church, except for the
purpose of discovering arguments in support of the
doctrines prescribed by Law; nor will he be allowed
to allege Scripture in defence of his published opinions
before an Ecclesiastical Court any more than he will
be allowed to allege reason and truth. " In investi-

gating the justice of such a charge," said the Privy
Council, in Bardon v. Heath, "we are bound to look
solely to the Statute and to the Articles. It would
be a departure from our duty if we were to admit any
discussion as to the conformity or nonconformity of the
Articles of Religion, or any of them, with the Holy
Scriptures." Who would be so infatuated as to take
the pretended conclusions of theologians placed under
such conditions as these for a new assurance of his
faith? And the case is the same with regard to the
former as it is with regard to the existing writers of
the Established Church : no assurance or comfort can
be derived in our present perplexities from any of them,
however great their learning, acuteness, and eloquence,
for the plain reason that on every doubtful question
of real moment their lips were sealed by law. Nor, it
is to be feared, will a clergyman do anything but
mischief, either to himself or to the community, by
desperately wrestling with legal obligations, and attempt-
ing to exercise a right of inquiry, which the pretended
inquirer has renounced, and which the law denies.
The reasonings of writers so fettered must, from the
nature of the case, be hesitating and their language
dark ; they must deal more in suggestion than in
plain statement : yet, from their position, they will
always be taken to mean much more than they say ;
and their works consequently are sure to scatter suspicion and distress without settling any question of
which they treat, and to produce at once the greatest
possible amount of irritation and the smallest possible amount of conviction. Even if a few real

loopholes are discovered in the law as the result of
the, suits to which such attempts give rise, these
loopholes, being merely accidental, and the result of
ignorance or oversight on the part of the legislator,
are of little value for the broad purposes of inquiry ;
while the struggle to make them available is a waste
of generous effort, which should be directed not to
obtaining loopholes for a few, but to obtaining an
open door for all*. It may at least be said, however, of
these persons, that their conduct, which inevitably exposes
them to obloquy and exclusion from preferment, is
not only disinterested but self-sacrificing in the highest
degree. The same can hardly be said of those who
take advantage of the state of the market afforded
by these disturbances to vend theological drugs com-
pounded of immoral ingredients, as antidotes to the
spirit of truth working in the hearts of men, through
doubt, to a better and more enduring faith. But even
these drugs, the object of which is to deaden particular
misgivings, are by one degree less noxious in their
practical effects than the attempt, for which the Oxford
school of theology is peculiarly responsible, to crush
all conscientious inquiry by arguments tending to
universal scepticism, and to prevent the promulgation

---

* In its recent and memorable decision in the case of Mr. Wilson,
the Privy Council has not departed from the principle that the clergy
of the Established Church are bound to teach the doctrines prescribed
by law, not the Gospel or the truth. That decision has indeed made a
'loophole' of the most tremendous kind. It has in effect left the code
of Anglican doctrine without any assignable foundation. But all parts
of the code (even the damnatory clauses of the Athanasian Creed) remain just as obligatory as before. [Note to 2nd ed.]

of inconvenient truths by teaching the world to despair
of truth. Yet works affecting to prove that men
cannot know God, and, by necessary implication, that
God cannot make Himself known to man, have been
applauded by the enemies of religious inquiry as
memorable apologies for the Christian revelation.

Nor does it seem possible to confer the power of
free inquiry which the age requires on the theologians
of the Established Church. Sir Stephen Lushington
says, that if further liberty is needed recourse must
be had to the Legislature, which established the
Articles and the Book of Common Prayer. But the
Legislature which established the Articles and the
Book of Common Prayer no longer exists. That
Legislature was an exclusively Anglican legislature,
which might, without flagrant incongruity, make laws
for the Anglican communion. It has passed away :
and in its place there now sits a mixed assembly
of Anglicans, Nonconformists, Roman Catholics, and
Jews. A reformation of the Anglican code of doctrine
by such a Legislature as this is more than minds
the most tolerant of logical inconsistencies could be
brought to endure ; not to mention that any recourse
to the Legislature would at once lay bare to the eyes
of all men the real foundation of the Anglican faith,
now hidden from the vulgar by the incrustations of
a respectable antiquity. The Established Church has
in fact drifted from her moorings in history to an
alien shore. The general system of which she was
a part has broken up, and she remains, the creature
of the Tudor Kings and Parliaments, surviving the

authors of her being, and with her only power of legislation and self-adaptation buried in their grave. So insuperable does this obstacle seem that it is superfluous to discuss other difficulties. We need not inquire whether it would be possible to bring the different parties in the Church to an agreement as to the degree of liberty to be conceded; whether, in fact, after abandoning the present limit it would be possible, in the face of the flood of pent-up desire for liberty which would break forth the moment the gates began to open, to fix a limit anywhere else; or whether an Established Church without a fixed limit of doctrine would be anything but an established chaos.

Under these circumstances it would seem that the free study of Theology in the Universities might possibly supply, in some measure at least, a pressing need which it is scarcely possible to supply in any other way. There, if anywhere, we might expect the study to be pursued with competent learning and with a due feeling of responsibility : and it would be pursued in immediate conjunction with Physical Science and Philosophy, with the conclusions of which it is the most pressing duty of the real theologian at the present juncture to reconcile religion. In order to set the study of Theology in the University free, it would be requisite, of course, to abolish the University Statute which confines the theological faculty to clergymen of the Established Church, but still more requisite to take from the authorities their legal power of punishing or harassing any member of the University on account of his religious opinions. To pretend that this measure would afford a panacea for the religious malady of the age would be ridiculous : but it would at least tend to substitute the serious study of our theological difficulties by learned and religious men for the reckless diffusion of scepticism by the unlearned and irreligious. It must be admitted that it would cause at first something of a shock : but that shock would certainly not be greater than those which are caused by manifestations of doubt and disquietude of conscience, some of them emanating from clergymen, of the cessation of which there is no prospect whatever ; while the knowledge that inquiry conducted through trustworthy organs was on foot, would in itself calm men's minds and dispose them to wait patiently for the result.

The study of theology in Oxford would then regain a real importance. At present, though sumptuously endowed, it confessedly languishes, not through the fault of the teachers, on whom the blame is commonly laid, but because nothing can be taught but Anglican or Patristic Divinity and Ecclesiastical History ; the great and vital questions of the day and the most influential works on the subject being necessarily excluded from view. No study pursued under such conditions could fail to sink into impotence and contempt. The professors of theology at the Universities have been called professors of an extinct science. It might be ⌐aid, with more truth, that they are at this moment professors debarred from treating of their science ; the scholastic science of theology having passed away, while the theology which investigates instead of dogmatising, (the foundations of which are beginning to be laid, though at present under rather sinister auspices,) is interdicted to the teachers of the Established Church. We shall be told at once that if free inquiry were permitted, our professors and students would all become sceptics. Of course, if you think fit to institute a free inquiry, you must resign yourself to the result. But to say that free inquiry, carried on by learned and conscientious men, must necessarily lead to sceptical conclusions, would be rash, since it would be equivalent to saying that sceptical conclusions must be true.

The University of Oxford has done much, both as an organ of mere repression, and as an organ of Romanizing speculation, to destroy the faith of the nation: let her now, as an organ of rational and conscientious inquiry, do something to restore it.

The theological lectures of the college tutors would of course not be affected by the removal of the restrictions on the free study of the subject in the University; they, and everything that depends on them, would remain as before. Nor does there seem any reason to apprehend that their character would be injuriously influenced by the presence of free inquiry in the University, any more than it is by the presence of books containing the results of free inquiry in the University and College libraries, in the booksellers' shops, and on the shelves of the tutors. As to the theological professorships, the five of most importance are attached to canonries of Christ Church, which constitute their endowment, and are therefore necessarily held by ecclesiastics: while the professor of Exegesis is elected by the Heads of Colleges, almost all of whom must be in Holy Orders. The emancipation of the study from restrictions prohibiting inquiries which might lead to truth is the only alteration in the existing state of things which it is proposed to make : and if truth is the first object, it is difficult to see on what ground such a prayer could be refused.

Let it be once more observed, in conclusion, that the point of view from which we have here endeavoured to regard the subject is that of the statesman, bound, in whatever he does, to look to the interest of the whole community, not of one party or Church alone. Arguments, therefore, based on the exclusive interest of an ecclesiastical party, or even of a particular Church, would not be relevant in reply.

Perhaps a word may be added by way of appeal to those whose sympathies are on the side of emancipation, but who sit silent when the question is before the House of Commons, thinking it hopeless to move because we are in the midst of a conservative reaction. That we are in the midst of a conservative reaction is unquestionable. Its signs, grotesque as well as grave, are visible on all sides, in the comic as well as in the serious press, in the affected passion of literary men for prize-fighting, as well as in the defeats of the liberal party at the elections, and in the passing of new game-laws by the House of Commons. And this reaction has produced a government having a not very remote analogy in its character to the governments of the great reaction in the time of

Charles II, and sustaining itself to a great extent by analogous means. But surely not much reflection is required to distinguish this back stream of opinion, however rapid for the moment, and whatever strange relics of the past it may bear upon its surface, from the main current; or to assign its temporary causes, and, with them, the proximate limits .of its existence. The lassitude and satiety which ensue after great political efforts, such as those which carried the Reform Bill and the Repeal of the Corn Laws, and the sudden influx of wealth among the governing classes, arising from railways, free trade, and prosperous speculation, which for the moment gives an ascendency to material interests, will, when taken together, go very far to account for all that we see; and neither of these causes is of a permanent kind. Scepticism has of course found its way into political as well as into religious life, enfeebling the character of political chiefs, and making political parties mistrustful of their principles and of the future. It happens, moreover, that the popular party in this country is at the present moment under the guidance of an isolated group of aristocratic leaders, whose original connection with it was merely accidental, whose objects and convictions were, in most cases, exhausted when they had carried the Reform Bill, and put an end to their own exclusion from power; and who, if they have brought forward popular measures since that time, have brought them forward less from a sincere desire of carrying them, than to oust the Conservatives from office. An analogous and incomparably more violent reaction has taken place, mainly as a consequence of overstrained political effort, in France; its symptoms, even down to the revival of barbarous amusements, being nearly the same, while it has produced a government highly congenial in its character, as we have abundant reason to know, to the reactionary government of this country. In both countries alike the chief of the political reaction, though notoriously indifferent himself to religious questions, has found and sought allies and supporters of his power among the reactionary clergy; and each country has seen the unnatural, or perhaps the natural, union of the least austere men of the world with the most pharisaical leaders of religious party and their organs. But no one, looking over the history of Europe during the last half century, or even to the general state of things at the present moment, can doubt in which direction the main stream of opinion flows. Even in France the reactionary force begins to give signs of exhaustion; while in England the great organs of public opinion, though the personal sympathies of their managers may be on the side of reaction, still do an unwilling homage to principles which are rooted in the deep convictions of the nation, and which will not fail, as soon as a real appeal is made to them, to respond to that appeal, and bring the reaction to an end. If the terrible strain laid on free institutions in America by the revolt of the Slaveowners has contributed to the prevailing mistrust of freedom, it now appears that free institutions will probably stand the strain,

and that this cause of reaction also will cease
to operate. We are told by politicians that when
the present Government expires, a Conservative
Government will certainly succeed to power. Be it
so. A government acting upon principle of any
kind is more congenial and more advantageous to
Liberalism, if Liberalism be sound, than cynical indifference. The tone of politics will be restored; and
we can no more apprehend a repeal of any of the great
liberal measures which have already been passed than
we can apprehend that prize-fights will actually be
legalized by Parliament, and celebrated under the
patronage of the Queen. Whatever ministers come
into office will find themselves placed, as before, at a
point, not alterable at their will, in the great movement
of transition through which society is passing from
its mediæval to its modern state. They will find
themselves, the moment the public mind has recovered
its tone, compelled to deal with the great problems
which that transition involves—the problem of ele-
vating the labouring class from their mediæval position
of serfdom to that of full and enfranchised members
of a real community, and the still more momentous
problem of transferring the basis of religion, on which
all society rests, from mediæval authority to conviction
the result of free inquiry and of liberty of conscience.
Already a great economical question, closely connected
with the first of these problems—the question of the
land-laws as affecting the distribution of land—has
begun to assume a practical aspect, and to gain a hold,
which it will never loose, upon the public mind. Other

symptoms of a change present themselves. The head
of the reactionary Government lives almost avowedly
from hand to mouth, sustaining himself by any support he can obtain for the moment, no matter from
what quarter; and anxious only to stifle all great
questions, the agitation of which, however essential
to the ultimate welfare and to the ultimate peace of
the country, might possibly interfere with his undis-
turbed possession of power for the remainder of his
term. But the debate on the Petition for the Aboli-
lition of Tests in the House of Commons showed that
there were some among the younger public men
disposed to look forward, and conscious that, though
the Government and its views might be ephemeral,
for them and their country there was still a political
future. If these men will embark in the cause of
Religious Emancipation, they may be assured, at least,
that it is no languid or fitful wave upon which their
political fortunes will be borne. It is the mighty and
irresistible tide of the Reformation, which, after being
arrested for three centuries by the great combined
powers of political and ecclesiastical reaction, has once
more begun to flow, and which will not cease flowing
till it has buried beneath its waves the last of the
restraints which a false authority has imposed on the
Christian conscience,—the last of the barriers which
political Churches have reared in the way of the reconciliation of Christendom.

The Academic Profession

An Arno Press Collection

Annan, Noel Gilroy. **Leslie Stephen:** His Thought and Character in Relation to His Time. 1952

Armytage, W. H. G. **Civic Universities:** Aspects of a British Tradition. 1955

Berdahl, Robert O. **British Universities and the State.** 1959

Bleuel, Hans Peter. **Deutschlands Bekenner** (German Men of Knowledge). 1968

Bowman, Claude Charleton. **The College Professor in America.** 1938

Busch, Alexander. **Die Geschichte des Privatdozenten** (History of Privat-Docentens). 1959

Caplow, Theodore and Reece J. McGee. **The Academic Marketplace.** 1958

Carnegie Foundation for the Advancement of Teaching. **The Financial Status of the Professor in America and in Germany.** 1908

Cattell, J. McKeen. **University Control.** 1913

Cheyney, Edward Potts. **History of the University of Pennsylvania:** 1740-1940. 1940

Elliott, Orrin Leslie. **Stanford University:** The First Twenty-Five Years. 1937

Ely, Richard T. **Ground Under Our Feet:** An Autobiography. 1938

Flach, Johannes. **Der Deutsche Professor der Gegenwart** (The German Professor Today). 1886

Hall, G. Stanley. **Life and Confessions of a Psychologist.** 1924

Hardy, G[odfrey] H[arold]. **Bertrand Russell & Trinity:** A College Controversy of the Last War. 1942

Kluge, Alexander. **Die Universitäts-Selbstverwaltung** (University Self-Government). 1958

Kotschnig, Walter M. **Unemployment in the Learned Professions.** 1937

Lazarsfeld, Paul F. and Wagner Thielens, Jr. **The Academic Mind:** Social Scientists in a Time of Crisis. 1958

McLaughlin, Mary Martin. **Intellectual Freedom and Its Limitations in the University of Paris in the Thirteenth and Fourteenth Centuries.** 1977

Metzger, Walter P., editor. **The American Concept of Academic Freedom in Formation:** A Collection of Essays and Reports. 1977

Metzger, Walter P., editor. **The Constitutional Status of Academic Freedom.** 1977

Metzger, Walter P., editor. **The Constitutional Status of Academic Tenure.** 1977

Metzger, Walter P., editor. **Professors on Guard:** The First AAUP Investigations. 1977

Metzger, Walter P., editor. **Reader on the Sociology of the Academic Profession.** 1977

Mims, Edwin. **History of Vanderbilt University.** 1946

Neumann, Franz L., et al. **The Cultural Migration:** The European Scholar in America. 1953

Nitsch, Wolfgang, et al. **Hochschule in der Demokratie** (The University in a Democracy). 1965

Pattison, Mark. **Suggestions on Academical Organization with Especial Reference to Oxford.** 1868

Pollard, Lucille Addison. **Women on College and University Faculties:** A Historical Survey and a Study of Their Present Academic Status. 1977

Proctor, Mortimer R. **The English University Novel.** 1957

Quincy, Josiah. **The History of Harvard University.** Two vols. 1840

Ross, Edward Alsworth. **Seventy Years of It:** An Autobiography. 1936

Rudy, S. Willis. **The College of the City of New York:** A History, 1847-1947. 1949

Slosson, Edwin E. **Great American Universities.** 1910

Smith, Goldwin. **A Plea for the Abolition of Tests in the University of Oxford.** 1864

Willey, Malcolm W. **Depression, Recovery and Higher Education:** A Report by Committee Y of the American Association of University Professors. 1937

Winstanley, D. A. **Early Victorian Cambridge.** 1940

Winstanley, D. A. **Later Victorian Cambridge.** 1947

Winstanley, D. A. **Unreformed Cambridge.** 1935

Yeomans, Henry Aaron. **Abbott Lawrence Lowell: 1856-1943.** 1948